Touch Key

10-Key Touch Key

Developing Speed and Accuracy

Jo Burton

David Burton

D1603499

PEARSON

Prentice Hall

Upper Saddle River, New Jersey
Columbus, Ohio

Senior Acquisitions Editor: Gary Bauer
Editorial Assistant: Jacqueline Knapke
Production Editor: Louise N. Sette
Design Coordinator: Diane Ernsberger
Cover Designer: Linda Sorrells-Smith
Production Manager: Pat Tonneman
Marketing Coordinator: Leigh Ann Sims

This book was printed and bound by Banta Book Group. The cover was printed by Phoenix Color Corp..

Pearson Education Ltd.
Pearson Education Singapore Pte. Ltd.
Pearson Education Canada, Ltd.
Pearson Education—Japan
Pearson Education Australia Pty. Limited
Pearson Education North Asia Ltd.
Pearson Educación de Mexico, S.A. de C.V.
Pearson Education Malaysia Pte. Ltd.

10 11 12 V036 12 11 10

ISBN 0-13-170363-3

Acknowledgments

Our sincere thanks to Janis Rollins, Caroline Garrett, and Mark Henry of Victoria College for their support and encouragement during the creation of this project and for their input during the testing of this software. Thanks also to Gary Bauer, Michelle Churma, and Joan Schramek for their unfailing help and advice.

Contents

PART 3 - MORE APPLYING YOUR TEN-KEY SKILL
USING THE WINDOWS CALCULATOR

PART 4 - MORE APPLYING YOUR TEN-KEY SKILL
COMPLETING SPREADSHEETS

Preface

The purpose of this textbook and software package is to facilitate the teaching of 10-key by touch using computer-assisted instruction and the computer numberpad. The student is then introduced to the desktop calculator. Next, the student is introduced to the Windows® calculator. Finally, the student may use the 10-key skills he has learned to enter data in partially completed spreadsheets using Excel® software.

Touch Key is a Windows® program. It is compatible with Windows 95/98/2000/ME/XP/NT. It features attractive, colorful screens. Students and instructors will find the program easy to use.

Touch Key is designed to teach 10-key by touch using the computer numberpad. Computer-assisted instruction allows for unlimited repetitions of exercises and for instant feedback.

The software provides Lessons, Drills, and Tests. Speed and accuracy are calculated and provided for each.

Actual keystrokes may be printed upon the completion of each lesson, drill, and test for diagnostic purposes. Keyed answers containing errors are marked with asterisks.

Timing bars appear on screens to give students an idea of their progress during timed lessons, drills, and tests.

Checkmarks in the pulldown menus indicate which activities have been completed.

Logs containing scores for Lessons, Drills, and Tests may be printed at any time. In addition, individual logs containing scores for Drills 1–6 may be printed. It is recommended that scores be printed on a regular basis in case of disk failure.

An introduction to the desktop calculator is included in the text, along with exercises and drills to provide students with additional 10-key practice.

An introduction to the Windows Calculator is also included in the text, along with several business problems to be solved using the Windows Calculator.

Several partially completed spreadsheet files are included to allow the student to obtain experience in entering numeric data in spreadsheets.

How Software is Supplied

A Touch Key CD and the 10-Key Touch key textbook are packaged together. The text includes instructions for using software, an introduction to the desktop calculator, and introduction to the Windows® calculator, and the data entry in spreadsheet exercises. An Instructor's Manual is also available.

System Requirements

- Intel 486 processor or equivalent
- 16 Meg RAM (32 Meg recommended)
- VGA (640 x 480) or SVGA (800 x 600) 256 color or higher
- CD-ROM Drive (Installation only)
- 3 meg available (Drive C)
- Windows 95, 98, 2000, ME, XP, or NT
- Windows Excel is required for completion of spreadsheet exercises
- 3.5 inch drive
- 3.5 inch formatted diskette

Installation Instructions

Note: It is recommended that all other Windows applications be closed before installing Touch Key.

1.   Press START on the Windows Taskbar.
2.   Choose RUN.
3.   Type D:\Setup.exe (where D represents your CDROM drive).
4.   Touch Key installation will begin. Follow instructions on screen.
5.   Restart your computer if prompted to do so.
6.   Touch Key setup is now complete.

PART 1

DEVELOPING YOUR TEN-KEY SKILL

Using Touch Key
10-Key Software

Getting Started

Before starting Touch Key, make sure your computer display is set properly. Select Start, Settings, Control Panel, Display, Settings. Change color palette to 256 color or higher. Change desktop to (640 x 480) or (800 x 600) pixels. Click OK and Yes to accept changes.

Also, check that the correct default printer is selected. Select Start, Settings, Printers. Right click the appropriate printer icon, select Set as Default, if necessary.

Why Use Touch Key?

The purpose of this program is to help you to enter numbers, including negative and decimal numbers, by touch on the numberpad of a computer keyboard. Whenever entering data on computers, accuracy is extremely important; therefore, accuracy as well as speed is encouraged.

Software written to accept numeric data has built-in formulas for necessary calculations and formatting. Usually, a number is simply keyed in the appropriate blank data field, followed by pressing the Enter key. Decimals are keyed, but not commas.

After learning to key numbers by touch, you will apply what you have learned to data entry jobs such as inventory ordering and payroll.

These skills may then be applied while using a desktop calculator, the Windows calculator, and by entering data in spreadsheets.

The Computer Numberpad

The numberpad on a computer has two kinds of keys: number keys and arithmetic operation keys (see **Figure 1**). These keys are used by turning NumLock on and pressing the keys on the numberpad. The following table identifies the arithmetic operation keys, describes what each does, and lists the symbols used to identify the keys (see **Table 1**).

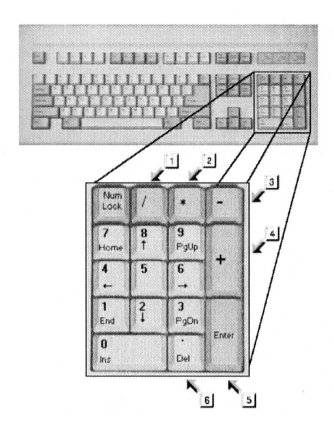

Figure 1

	Operation	Symbol	Description
1	Division	/	Division
2	Multiplication	*	Multiplication
3	Subtraction	-	Subtraction
4	Addition	+	Addition
5	Total	Enter	May be used to enter data which has been keyed or to complete an arithmetic operation
6	Decimal	. Del	Enters a decimal into the number

Table 1

Preparing to 10-Key by Touch

Organization of Workspace

Adjust your chair and keyboard. Position the keyboard so that the J key is centered in front of your body. The edge of the keyboard should be at the edge of the table or desk.

Sit with your feet flat on the floor. Lean forward slightly. Your arm should hang comfortably at your side from shoulder to elbow. Raise your right hand, curl your fingers, and poise them over the numberpad.

Keystroking Technique

Home Row. The 4, 5, and 6 keys are the home row keys on a numberpad. Curl the fingers of the right hand. Place the index finger on the 4 key, the middle finger on the 5 key, and the ring finger on the 6 key. The 5 key has a small raised dot or bar on its surface to help you identify it by touch.

Figure 2 The Home Row Keys

Refer to **Figure 2** for correct hand position on the home row. Notice that the fingers are in position to strike the home row keys with a straight downward motion. The wrist is straight. To correctly key the home row keys, visualize a small hammer striking a tack. Your fingers should deliver the same sharp rap on the home row keys as a hammer on a tack.

Figure 3 The Seven Key

Top Row. Strike the upper row keys with the pad or fleshy part of the finger (see **Figure 3**). After striking a key on the top row, return your finger to the appropriate key on the home row. The 4 (index) finger reaches upward to strike the 7 key, the 5 finger strikes the 8 key, and the 6 finger strikes the 9 key.

Figure 4 The One Key

Bottom Row. Strike the keys on the bottom row with the fingernail portion of the fingertips, and then return the finger to the home row. Strike the 1 key with the 4 finger, strike the 2 key with the 5 finger, and strike the 3 key with the 6 finger (**Figure 4**).

The Zero Key and Decimal Key. Strike the 0 key with the thumb of the right hand. Strike the decimal key with the ring or 6 finger.

Figure 5 The Enter Key

The Enter Key, + Key, and − Key. Strike the enter key (see **Figure 5**), plus sign (**Figure 6**) and minus sign (**Figure 7**) with the little finger.

Figure 6 The Plus Key

Figure 7 The Minus Key

A pencil may be held in the crease of the thumb and right hand when it is necessary to record results of calculations on a paper copy (**Figure 8**).

Figure 8 Holding the Pencil

Organization of Touch Key Lessons, Drills, and Tests

The following chart outlines the content of each Lesson and Drill and the order in which the drills, lessons and tests should be attempted. If this outline is followed, you will practice each key before you encounter that key in a drill or test. Thus, you are assured of "no surprises."

Content of Touch Key Lessons, Drills, and Tests in Suggested Completion Order
Lesson 1—Home row keys and Enter key, 3-digit numbers
Lesson 2—Top row keys, 3-digit numbers
Lesson 3—Bottom row keys, 3-digit numbers
Lesson 4—4, 5, 6, 7, 8, and 9 keys, 3-digit numbers
Lesson 5—1, 2, 3, 4, 5, and 6 keys, 3-digit numbers
Lesson 6—1 through 9 keys, 3-digit numbers
Lesson 7—1 through 9 keys and 0 key, 3-digit numbers
Drill 1—0 through 9 keys, 3-digit numbers
Lesson 8—0 through 9 keys, 4-digit numbers
Drill 2—0 through 9 keys, 4-digit numbers
Lesson 9—0 through 9 keys, 5-digit numbers
Drill 3—0 through 9 keys, 5-digit numbers
Lesson 10—0 through 9 keys and decimal key, 6-digit numbers
Drill 4—0 through 9 keys and decimal key, 6-digit numbers
Lesson 11—0 through 9 keys, decimal key and minus key, 6-digit numbers
Drill 5—0 through 9 keys, decimal key and minus key, 6-digit numbers
Drill 6—0 through 9 keys, 1- through 5-digit numbers (mixed)
Check Test
Order Test
Payroll Test
Invoice Test

Table 2

As you complete the following activities, record your speed and accuracy scores along with the date. It is suggested that you record the activity when an accuracy score of 95% or better is achieved. The numbers in parentheses indicate the number of minutes in each drill or test.

Student Lesson Log			
Activity	Speed	Accuracy	Date
(Lesson) 1A			
1B			
1C			
1D			
1E			
(Lesson) 2A			
2B			
2C			
2D			
2E			
(Lesson) 3A			
3B			
3C			
3D			
3E			
(Lesson) 4A			
4B			
4C			
4D			
4E			
(Lesson) 5A			
5B			
5C			
5D			
5E			
(Lesson) 6A			
6B			
6C			
6D			
6E			
(Lesson) 7A			
7B			
7C			
7D			
7E			
(Drill) 1A (1')			
1B (1')			

Student Lesson Log			
Activity	Speed	Accuracy	Date
1C (1')			
1D (1')			
1E (1')			
1 (3')			
1 (5')			
(Lesson) 8A			
8B			
8C			
8D			
8E			
(Drill) 2A (1')			
2B (1')			
2C (1')			
2D (1')			
2E (1')			
2 (3')			
2 (5')			
(Lesson) 9A			
9B			
9C			
9D			
9E			
(Drill) 3A (1')			
3B (1')			
3C (1')			
3D (1')			
3E (1')			
3 (3')			
3 (5')			
(Lesson) 10A			
10B			
10C			
10D			
10E			
(Drill) 4A (1')			
4B (1')			
4C (1')			
4D (1')			
4E (1')			
4 (3')			
4 (5')			

Student Lesson Log			
Activity	Speed	Accuracy	Date
(Lesson) 11A			
11B			
11C			
11D			
11E			
(Drill) 5A (1')			
5B (1')			
5C (1')			
5D (1')			
5E (1')			
5 (3')			
5 (5')			
(Drill) 6A (1')			
6B (1')			
6C (1')			
6D (1')			
6E (1')			
6 (3')			
6 (5')			
(Test) Checks (8')*			
(Test) Order (5')**			
(Test) Payroll (10')*			
(Test) Invoice (12')*			

Table 3

*These tests require printed materials contained in this text.

**This test does not require printed materials.

As you attain the following speed for each lesson, enter the date and the percent of accuracy.

Example: On the day you reach 6000 strokes per hour for Lesson 1, enter the date and the percent of accuracy in the cell located beside Lesson 1 under 6000.

Speed Progress Chart for Touch Key													
	6000	6500	7000	7500	8000	8500	9000	9500	10000	10500	11000	11500	12000
Lesson 1													
Lesson 2													
Lesson 3													
Lesson 4													
Lesson 5													
Lesson 6													
Lesson 7													
Drill 1													
Lesson 8													
Drill 2													
Lesson 9													
Drill 3													
Lesson 10													
Drill 4													
Lesson 11													
Drill 5													
Drill 6													
Check Test													
Order Test													
Payroll Test													
Invoice Test													

Table 4

Touch Key

Starting Touch Key

1. Select Start, Programs, Touch Key. The Touch Key startup screen will appear.

2. The FIRST time you use Touch Key, you will need to create a student data disk. Insert a blank, formatted disk in the floppy drive and select Create Data Disk.

3. With the student data disk in the floppy drive, select Start. You will need this disk each time you use Touch Key in order to have a record of your work.

4. On the Name, Course, and Password window type the requested information in the boxes provided (**Figure 9**).

    a. Type your name in the box, check it for accuracy, use the Backspace key to make necessary corrections, then press Enter.

Note: You will want to make sure your name is correct because it will display at the top of the screen the entire time the program is in use. Information on this Window may not be changed after the Enter key has been pressed in the Password box.

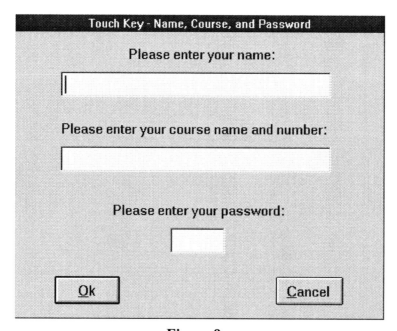

Figure 9

b. Type your course name and number as directed by your instructor. Check that you have typed it correctly before pressing Enter. This information will be displayed on all of your print jobs.

c. Type a password. The password may be nine letters or numbers in length. Do not use special characters or symbols. (If you use your Social Security number as your password, do not type hyphens.)

- REMEMBER YOUR PASSWORD. You will need it each time you start the program.

- KEEP YOUR PASSWORD **CONFIDENTIAL**.

5. The Startup window will reappear. Select Start. Next, the Login window (**Figure 10**) will appear which contains the name and course information as you entered it on the Student Name, Course, and Password window.

6. You will need to type your password again, EXACTLY as you entered it on the Name, Course, and Password window.

7. In the future, each time you start the Touch Key program you will need to supply only your password.

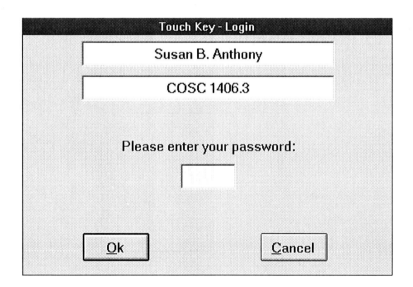

Figure 10

Exiting the Program

Always exit computer programs properly. Select Main Menu (if necessary), Exit. You should shut down the Windows software before turning the computer off. Check with your instructor for the specific lab procedure you should use.

Main Menu

The main menu contains the selections Lessons, Drills, Tests, Print, and Exit. Select the appropriate category to access a pulldown menu of options. **Figure 11** shows the Lessons pulldown menu and the Lesson 1 submenu. A checkmark indicates that an activity has been completed.

Lessons

Each of the eleven lessons has five components labeled A through E as shown in **Figure 11**. Each component of the lesson consists of fifty 3- to 6-digit numbers (problems) to be keyed. In each component, the number to be keyed appears in a white box. As you key, the numbers keyed will appear in a yellow box. Press the Enter key after each number. A progress bar is displayed so that you will have an indication of the number of problems remaining in the activity. Another aid will alert you when you reach the last problem to be keyed. The numbers to be keyed will turn red.

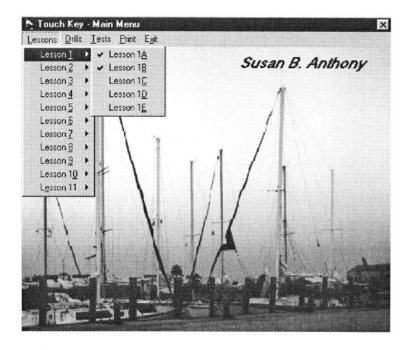

Figure 11

Numbers (problems) to be keyed will change with each repetition of the lesson component so that no two components will be alike. Therefore, with your instructor's approval, activities may be repeated as many times as desired in an attempt to improve your keystrokes.

You may correct errors in a number with the Backspace key BEFORE the Enter key is pressed. However, the time clock will be running, so each correction will cost you time. It is recommended that you NOT correct while keying Touch Key Lessons, because correcting is detrimental to creating an even keystroking technique and to building speed.

After the last problem has been entered, Lesson Results will be displayed. At this point, you may either Print or return to the Main Menu.

If Print is selected, the problems and your actual keystrokes will be printed on a report called Lesson Results. An asterisk placed beside the column of your keystrokes indicates errors. This is an important diagnostic tool. By comparing the two columns containing the problems and your keystrokes, you can identify troublesome keys.

Strokes per Hour, Total Errors, and Percent Accuracy are also printed on the Lesson Results report.

Note: It is important that you wait until the print job is finished and that you check for a successful print job before returning to the Main Menu. Once Main Menu has been selected, the actual keys strokes can no longer be printed.

However, Strokes per Hour, Errors, and Percent Accuracy are stored permanently in the Lesson Log on the student data disk and may be printed at any time. (This feature conserves disk space.) To print a Lesson Log, return to the Main Menu; select the Print menu, then Lesson Log.

Note: It is strongly recommended that you print Logs on a regular basis and either submit the printed logs to the instructor or retain them in a folder in case of computer or disk failure. All logs will be personalized with your name, course, current date, and current time for each lesson, drill, or test taken.

Drills

Six drills are included, which consist of timings in which you will use specified keys covered in the Lessons (see **Table 2**). Each drill has 5 components labeled A through E. You may choose 1, 3, or 5-minute timings at the Touch Key Timing Control window. You should complete five 1-minute timings, one 3-minute timing, and one 5-minute timing for each drill. (See the Student Lesson Log.) A picture of the numberpad keys will display on the screen. The keys to be practiced in the selected drill are marked with a red asterisk.

Features contained in the Lessons are also contained in the Drills. You will key the number that appears in the white box and press Enter. A progress bar will be displayed to give you an indication of the time remaining. When five seconds remain in the timing, the numbers to be keyed turn red to alert you that time is almost up.

After the drill, Strokes per Hour, Total Errors, and Percent Accuracy are displayed. At this point, you may print the drill, including your actual keystrokes and error indicators.

You should wait until the print job is finished and check for a successful print job before returning to the Main Menu. Once Main Menu has been selected, the actual keystrokes can no longer be printed. However, Strokes Per Hour, Total Errors, and Percent Accuracy are stored in the Drill Log on the student data disk and may be printed at any time.

Drills may be used as speed tests as well as speed-building exercises. Remember, no two drills are alike.

Tests

Several exercises are included to give you practice with production jobs. There are maximum time limits given for the applications. Strokes per Hour, Errors, and Percent Accuracy are calculated and stored in the Test Log and may be printed at any time. These tests may be used for practice or grading purposes. Check with your instructor.

Check Verification Test

Similar to work done in proofing departments of banks, in this test data must be entered from checks. Simulated checks will be used for this test. **Figure 12** shows the beginning window of the Check Verification Test.

Check Verification Instructions

Read the following set of instructions before beginning the test. The test may be canceled before the timing begins, but not after.

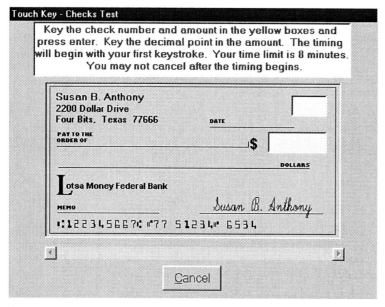

Figure 12

- In proofing checks, the operator must always read and key the spelled-out amount—not the amount written in figures. You will also follow this procedure.

- Decimals must be keyed in the amount.

- Be careful not to lose your place. Information must be keyed in correct order, check number first, then amount of check.

- It is possible to correct information in a box using the Backspace key. To move to a previous box press Shift + Tab. To move to the next box, press Tab. It is not possible to move to a previous screen, however.

- The maximum time limit for this test is 8 minutes. The timing will stop when all data has been entered or when the time limit has been reached, whichever comes first.

Strokes per Hour, Errors, and Percent Accuracy are given. The test and your actual keystrokes may be printed at this point. Scores may be printed at any time from the Test Log under Print on the Main menu.

Turn to the next page to begin the checks test.

Check 7766

Susan B. Anthony   **7766**
2200 Dollar Drive
Four Bits, Texas 77666   88-566/223

DATE *Feb. 5, 2001*

PAT TO THE
ORDER OF *Jessica Long* $ | 934.48 |

Nine hundred thirty-four dollars & 48/100   DOLLARS

Lotsa Money Federal Bank

MEMO   *Susan B. Anthony*

⑈1 2 2 3 4 5 6 6 7⑆ ⑆77 5 1 2 3 4⑈

Check 7767

Susan B. Anthony   **7767**
2200 Dollar Drive
Four Bits, Texas 77666   88-566/223

DATE *Feb. 5, 2001*

PAT TO THE
ORDER OF *Natalie Waits* $ | 152.48 |

One hundred fifty-two dollars & 48/100   DOLLARS

Lotsa Money Federal Bank

MEMO   *Susan B. Anthony*

⑈1 2 2 3 4 5 6 6 7⑆ ⑆77 5 1 2 3 4⑈

Check 7768

Susan B. Anthony   **7768**
2200 Dollar Drive
Four Bits, Texas 77666   88-566/223

DATE *Feb. 5, 2001*

PAT TO THE
ORDER OF *Mrs. Juan Velasquez* $ | 364.92 |

Three hundred sixty-four dollars & 92/100   DOLLARS

Lotsa Money Federal Bank

MEMO   *Susan B. Anthony*

⑈1 2 2 3 4 5 6 6 7⑆ ⑆77 5 1 2 3 4⑈

Check 7769

Susan B. Anthony
2200 Dollar Drive
Four Bits, Texas 77666

7769

88-566/223

DATE *Feb. 5, 2001*

PAT TO THE ORDER OF *Jennifer Dupree* $ | 19.15 |

Nineteen dollars & 15/100 DOLLARS

Lotsa Money Federal Bank

MEMO _____ *Susan B. Anthony*

⑈123456670 ⑈77 51234⑈

Check 7770

Susan B. Anthony
2200 Dollar Drive
Four Bits, Texas 77666

7770

88-566/223

DATE *Feb. 5, 2001*

PAT TO THE ORDER OF *Robert Ainsley* $ | 686.82 |

Six hundred eighty-six dollars & 82/100 DOLLARS

Lotsa Money Federal Bank

MEMO _____ *Susan B. Anthony*

⑈123456670 ⑈77 51234⑈

Check 7771

Susan B. Anthony
2200 Dollar Drive
Four Bits, Texas 77666

7771

88-566/223

DATE *Feb. 5, 2001*

PAT TO THE ORDER OF *Lacey Anderson* $ | 549.68 |

Five hundred forty-nine dollars & 68/100 DOLLARS

Lotsa Money Federal Bank

MEMO _____ *Susan B. Anthony*

⑈123456670 ⑈77 51234⑈

Susan B. Anthony   7772
2200 Dollar Drive
Four Bits, Texas 77666   DATE *Feb. 5, 2001* 88-566/223

PAT TO THE
ORDER OF *Julie Newman* $ 448.12

Four hundred forty-eight dollars & 12/100   DOLLARS

Lotsa Money Federal Bank

MEMO   *Susan B. Anthony*

⑆1223456670⑈77 51234⑇

Susan B. Anthony   7773
2200 Dollar Drive
Four Bits, Texas 77666   DATE *Feb. 5, 2001* 88-566/223

PAT TO THE
ORDER OF *Richard Nicks* $ 82.72

Eighty-two dollars & 72/100   DOLLARS

Lotsa Money Federal Bank

MEMO   *Susan B. Anthony*

⑆1223456670⑈77 51234⑇

Susan B. Anthony   7774
2200 Dollar Drive
Four Bits, Texas 77666   DATE *Feb. 5, 2001* 88-566/223

PAT TO THE
ORDER OF *Donna Albright* $ 102.24

One hundred two dollars & 24/100   DOLLARS

Lotsa Money Federal Bank

MEMO   *Susan B. Anthony*

⑆1223456670⑈77 51234⑇

Susan B. Anthony
2200 Dollar Drive
Four Bits, Texas 77666

7775

DATE *Feb. 5, 2001* 88-566/223

PAY TO THE ORDER OF *Allen Wade* $ | *539.15*

Five hundred thirty-nine dollars & 15/100 DOLLARS

Lotsa Money Federal Bank

MEMO _____ *Susan B. Anthony*

⑆123456673⑆ ⑈77 51234⑉

Susan B. Anthony
2200 Dollar Drive
Four Bits, Texas 77666

7776

DATE *Feb. 5, 2001* 88-566/223

PAY TO THE ORDER OF *Walter Smith* $ | *982.10*

Nine hundred eighty-two dollars & 10/100 DOLLARS

Lotsa Money Federal Bank

MEMO _____ *Susan B. Anthony*

⑆123456673⑆ ⑈77 51234⑉

Susan B. Anthony
2200 Dollar Drive
Four Bits, Texas 77666

7777

DATE *Feb. 5, 2001* 88-566/223

PAY TO THE ORDER OF *Wendel Holmes* $ | *871.08*

Eight hundred seventy-one dollars & 08/100 DOLLARS

Lotsa Money Federal Bank

MEMO _____ *Susan B. Anthony*

⑆123456673⑆ ⑈77 51234⑉

Susan B. Anthony   7778
2200 Dollar Drive
Four Bits, Texas 77666   DATE *Feb. 5, 2001*   88-566/223

PAT TO THE
ORDER OF *Oliver Tobar* $ | 631.13 |

Six hundred thirty-one dollars & 13/100   DOLLARS

L otsa Money Federal Bank

MEMO _____   *Susan B. Anthony*

⑆1 2 2 3 4 5 6 6 7⑆ ⑈77 5 1 2 3 4⑊

Susan B. Anthony   7779
2200 Dollar Drive
Four Bits, Texas 77666   DATE *Feb. 5, 2001*   88-566/223

PAT TO THE
ORDER OF *Andrew Johnson* $ | 555.72 |

Five hundred fifty-five dollars & 72/100   DOLLARS

L otsa Money Federal Bank

MEMO _____   *Susan B. Anthony*

⑆1 2 2 3 4 5 6 6 7⑆ ⑈77 5 1 2 3 4⑊

Susan B. Anthony   7780
2200 Dollar Drive
Four Bits, Texas 77666   DATE *Feb. 5, 2001*   88-566/223

PAT TO THE
ORDER OF *Annie Taylor* $ | 398.44 |

Three hundred ninety-eight dollars & 44/100 DOLLARS

L otsa Money Federal Bank

MEMO _____   *Susan B. Anthony*

⑆1 2 2 3 4 5 6 6 7⑆ ⑈77 5 1 2 3 4⑊

Check 7781

Susan B. Anthony
2200 Dollar Drive
Four Bits, Texas 77666

7781

88-566/223

DATE *Feb. 5, 2001*

PAY TO THE ORDER OF *Mrs. Elmer Jamison* $ *59.85*

Fifty-nine dollars & 85/100 DOLLARS

Lotsa Money Federal Bank

MEMO

Susan B. Anthony

⑆1 2 2 3 4 5 6 6 7⑆ ⑈7 7 5 1 2 3 4⑈

Check 7782

Susan B. Anthony
2200 Dollar Drive
Four Bits, Texas 77666

7782

88-566/223

DATE *Feb. 5, 2001*

PAY TO THE ORDER OF *Drew Leighton* $ *572.35*

Five hundred seventy-two dollars & 35/100 DOLLARS

Lotsa Money Federal Bank

MEMO

Susan B. Anthony

⑆1 2 2 3 4 5 6 6 7⑆ ⑈7 7 5 1 2 3 4⑈

Check 7783

Susan B. Anthony
2200 Dollar Drive
Four Bits, Texas 77666

7783

88-566/223

DATE *Feb. 5, 2001*

PAY TO THE ORDER OF *Lance Ferrel* $ *757.48*

Seven hundred fifty-seven dollars & 48/100 DOLLARS

Lotsa Money Federal Bank

MEMO

Susan B. Anthony

⑆1 2 2 3 4 5 6 6 7⑆ ⑈7 7 5 1 2 3 4⑈

Susan B. Anthony   7784
2200 Dollar Drive
Four Bits, Texas 77666   DATE *Feb. 5, 2001*   88-566/223

PAT TO THE
ORDER OF   *Linda Tennyson* $ 636.92

Six hundred thirty-six dollars & 92/100   DOLLARS

Lotsa Money Federal Bank

MEMO   *Susan B. Anthony*

⑈1223456678⑈ ⑈77 51234⑈

Susan B. Anthony   7785
2200 Dollar Drive
Four Bits, Texas 77666   DATE *Feb. 5, 2001*   88-566/223

PAT TO THE
ORDER OF   *Jane Dawson* $ 982.42

Nine hundred eighty-two dollars & 42/100   DOLLARS

Lotsa Money Federal Bank

MEMO   *Susan B. Anthony*

⑈1223456678⑈ ⑈77 51234⑈

Susan B. Anthony   7786
2200 Dollar Drive
Four Bits, Texas 77666   DATE *Feb. 5, 2001*   88-566/223

PAT TO THE
ORDER OF   *Darrell Welden* $ 564.97

Five hundred sixty-four dollars & 97/100   DOLLARS

Lotsa Money Federal Bank

MEMO   *Susan B. Anthony*

⑈1223456678⑈ ⑈77 51234⑈

Susan B. Anthony
2200 Dollar Drive
Four Bits, Texas 77666

7787

DATE *Feb. 5, 2001*

88-566/223

PAT TO THE ORDER OF *Danny Johnson*

$ *437.14*

Four hundred thirty-seven dollars & 14/100   DOLLARS

Lotsa Money Federal Bank

MEMO

Susan B. Anthony

⑆1 2 2 3 4 5 6 6 7⑆ ⑈77 5 1 2 3 4⑈

Susan B. Anthony
2200 Dollar Drive
Four Bits, Texas 77666

7788

DATE *Feb. 5, 2001*

88-566/223

PAT TO THE ORDER OF *Dana Smith*

$ *516.25*

Five hundred sixteen dollars & 25/100   DOLLARS

Lotsa Money Federal Bank

MEMO

Susan B. Anthony

⑆1 2 2 3 4 5 6 6 7⑆ ⑈77 5 1 2 3 4⑈

Susan B. Anthony
2200 Dollar Drive
Four Bits, Texas 77666

7789

DATE *Feb. 5, 2001*

88-566/223

PAT TO THE ORDER OF *John Johnson*

$ *669.71*

Six hundred sixty-nine dollars & 71/100   DOLLARS

Lotsa Money Federal Bank

MEMO

Susan B. Anthony

⑆1 2 2 3 4 5 6 6 7⑆ ⑈77 5 1 2 3 4⑈

Check 7790

Susan B. Anthony
2200 Dollar Drive
Four Bits, Texas 77666

7790

88-566/223

DATE *Feb. 5, 2001*

PAT TO THE ORDER OF *William Jones*

$ *444.41*

Four hundred forty-four dollars & 41/100   DOLLARS

Lotsa Money Federal Bank

MEMO _____

Susan B. Anthony

⑈1 2 2 3 4 5 6 6 7⑈ ⑈77 5 1 2 3 4⑈

Check 7791

Susan B. Anthony
2200 Dollar Drive
Four Bits, Texas 77666

7791

88-566/223

DATE *Feb. 5, 2001*

PAT TO THE ORDER OF *Janie Ireland*

$ *152.16*

One hundred fifty-two dollars & 16/100   DOLLARS

Lotsa Money Federal Bank

MEMO _____

Susan B. Anthony

⑈1 2 2 3 4 5 6 6 7⑈ ⑈77 5 1 2 3 4⑈

Check 7792

Susan B. Anthony
2200 Dollar Drive
Four Bits, Texas 77666

7792

88-566/223

DATE *Feb. 5, 2001*

PAT TO THE ORDER OF *Marilyn Rains*

$ *120.28*

One hundred twenty dollars & 28/100   DOLLARS

Lotsa Money Federal Bank

MEMO _____

Susan B. Anthony

⑈1 2 2 3 4 5 6 6 7⑈ ⑈77 5 1 2 3 4⑈

Check 7793

Susan B. Anthony
2200 Dollar Drive
Four Bits, Texas 77666

7793

88-566/223

DATE *Feb. 5, 2001*

PAT TO THE
ORDER OF *Clara Schiller* $ *191.11*

One hundred ninety-one dollars & 11/100   DOLLARS

Lotsa Money Federal Bank

MEMO _____   *Susan B. Anthony*

⑈123456673⑈ ⑈77 51234⑈

Check 7794

Susan B. Anthony
2200 Dollar Drive
Four Bits, Texas 77666

7794

88-566/223

DATE *Feb. 5, 2001*

PAT TO THE
ORDER OF *Ed Blakeney* $ *587.06*

Five hundred eighty-seven dollars & 06/100   DOLLARS

Lotsa Money Federal Bank

MEMO _____   *Susan B. Anthony*

⑈123456673⑈ ⑈77 51234⑈

Check 7795

Susan B. Anthony
2200 Dollar Drive
Four Bits, Texas 77666

7795

88-566/223

DATE *Feb. 5, 2001*

PAT TO THE
ORDER OF *Patsy Dillon* $ *353.69*

Three hundred fifty-three dollars & 69/100   DOLLARS

Lotsa Money Federal Bank

MEMO _____   *Susan B. Anthony*

⑈123456673⑈ ⑈77 51234⑈

Susan B. Anthony   7796
2200 Dollar Drive
Four Bits, Texas 77666   DATE *Feb. 5, 2001* ⁸⁸⁻⁵⁶⁶/²²³

PAT TO THE
ORDER OF *Terry Miller* $ 668.11

Six hundred sixty-eight dollars & 11/100   DOLLARS

L otsa Money Federal Bank

MEMO _____   *Susan B. Anthony*

⑈1 2 2 3 4 5 6 6 7⑈ ⑈77 5 1 2 3 4⑈

Susan B. Anthony   7797
2200 Dollar Drive
Four Bits, Texas 77666   DATE *Feb. 5, 2001* ⁸⁸⁻⁵⁶⁶/²²³

PAT TO THE
ORDER OF *Brenda J. Lee* $ 752.27

Seven hundred fifty-two dollars & 27/100   DOLLARS

L otsa Money Federal Bank

MEMO _____   *Susan B. Anthony*

⑈1 2 2 3 4 5 6 6 7⑈ ⑈77 5 1 2 3 4⑈

Susan B. Anthony   7798
2200 Dollar Drive
Four Bits, Texas 77666   DATE *Feb. 5, 2001* ⁸⁸⁻⁵⁶⁶/²²³

PAT TO THE
ORDER OF *Robert Brewster* $ 121.57

One hundred twenty-one dollars & 57/100   DOLLARS

L otsa Money Federal Bank

MEMO _____   *Susan B. Anthony*

⑈1 2 2 3 4 5 6 6 7⑈ ⑈77 5 1 2 3 4⑈

Check 7799

Susan B. Anthony
2200 Dollar Drive
Four Bits, Texas 77666

7799

DATE *Feb. 5, 2001* 88-566/223

PAT TO THE
ORDER OF *Terry M. Albright* $ 119.19

One hundred nineteen dollars & 19/100 DOLLARS

Lotsa Money Federal Bank

MEMO _____   *Susan B. Anthony*

⑂123456 67⑂ ⑈77 51234⑇

Check 7800

Susan B. Anthony
2200 Dollar Drive
Four Bits, Texas 77666

7800

DATE *Feb. 5, 2001* 88-566/223

PAT TO THE
ORDER OF *David Lassiter* $ 828.81

Eight hundred twenty-eight dollars & 81/100 DOLLARS

Lotsa Money Federal Bank

MEMO _____   *Susan B. Anthony*

⑂123456 67⑂ ⑈77 51234⑇

Check 7801

Susan B. Anthony
2200 Dollar Drive
Four Bits, Texas 77666

7801

DATE *Feb. 5, 2001* 88-566/223

PAT TO THE
ORDER OF *Ben Brown* $ 911.19

Nine hundred eleven dollars & 19/100 DOLLARS

Lotsa Money Federal Bank

MEMO _____   *Susan B. Anthony*

⑂123456 67⑂ ⑈77 51234⑇

Susan B. Anthony   7802
2200 Dollar Drive
Four Bits, Texas 77666   DATE *Feb. 5, 2001* 88-566/223

PAT TO THE
ORDER OF *Betty Patton* $ 343.19

Three hundred forty-three dollars & 19/100   DOLLARS

Lotsa Money Federal Bank

MEMO   *Susan B. Anthony*

⑆122345667⑆ ⑈77 51234⑆

Susan B. Anthony   7803
2200 Dollar Drive
Four Bits, Texas 77666   DATE *Feb. 5, 2001* 88-566/223

PAT TO THE
ORDER OF *Veronica Quinonez* $ 952.93

Nine hundred fifty-two dollars & 93/100   DOLLARS

Lotsa Money Federal Bank

MEMO   *Susan B. Anthony*

⑆122345667⑆ ⑈77 51234⑆

Susan B. Anthony   7804
2200 Dollar Drive
Four Bits, Texas 77666   DATE *Feb. 5, 2001* 88-566/223

PAT TO THE
ORDER OF *Larry Roberts* $ 59.46

Fifty-nine dollars & 46/100   DOLLARS

Lotsa Money Federal Bank

MEMO   *Susan B. Anthony*

⑆122345667⑆ ⑈77 51234⑆

Susan B. Anthony   7805
2200 Dollar Drive
Four Bits, Texas 77666   DATE _Feb. 5, 2001_ 88-566/223

PAT TO THE
ORDER OF   _Jim Ramirez_ $ |559.66|

Five hundred fifty-nine dollars & 66/100   DOLLARS

Lotsa Money Federal Bank

MEMO _____   _Susan B. Anthony_

⑆1234566⑇7⑆ ⑈77 51234⑈

Susan B. Anthony   7806
2200 Dollar Drive
Four Bits, Texas 77666   DATE _Feb. 5, 2001_ 88-566/223

PAT TO THE
ORDER OF   _Donald Beck_ $ |172.36|

One hundred seventy-two dollars & 36/100   DOLLARS

Lotsa Money Federal Bank

MEMO _____   _Susan B. Anthony_

⑆1234566⑇7⑆ ⑈77 51234⑈

Susan B. Anthony   7807
2200 Dollar Drive
Four Bits, Texas 77666   DATE _Feb. 5, 2001_ 88-566/223

PAT TO THE
ORDER OF   _Mark Blocker_ $ |457.96|

Four hundred fifty seven dollars & 96/100   DOLLARS

Lotsa Money Federal Bank

MEMO _____   _Susan B. Anthony_

⑆1234566⑇7⑆ ⑈77 51234⑈

10-Key Touch Key   **31**

Check 7808

Susan B. Anthony
2200 Dollar Drive
Four Bits, Texas 77666

7808

88-566/223

DATE *Feb. 5, 2001*

PAY TO THE ORDER OF *Peter Haus* $ **14.49**

Fourteen dollars & 49/100 DOLLARS

Lotsa Money Federal Bank

MEMO _____ *Susan B. Anthony*

⑆1 2 2 3 4 5 6 6 7⑆ ⑈77 5 1 2 3 4⑈

Check 7809

Susan B. Anthony
2200 Dollar Drive
Four Bits, Texas 77666

7809

88-566/223

DATE *Feb. 5, 2001*

PAY TO THE ORDER OF *Julie Tineman* $ **882.29**

Eight hundred eighty-two dollars & 29/100 DOLLARS

Lotsa Money Federal Bank

MEMO _____ *Susan B. Anthony*

⑆1 2 2 3 4 5 6 6 7⑆ ⑈77 5 1 2 3 4⑈

Check 7810

Susan B. Anthony
2200 Dollar Drive
Four Bits, Texas 77666

7810

88-566/223

DATE *Feb. 5, 2001*

PAY TO THE ORDER OF *Kathy Leiberman* $ **164.19**

One hundred sixty-four dollars & 19/100 DOLLARS

Lotsa Money Federal Bank

MEMO _____ *Susan B. Anthony*

⑆1 2 2 3 4 5 6 6 7⑆ ⑈77 5 1 2 3 4⑈

Susan B. Anthony   7811
2200 Dollar Drive
Four Bits, Texas 77666   DATE *Feb. 5, 2001*   88-566/223

PAT TO THE
ORDER OF *Veronica Landen* $ | 535.16 |

Five hundred thirty-five dollars & 16/100   DOLLARS

Lotsa Money Federal Bank

MEMO _____   *Susan B. Anthony*

⑈1 2 2 3 4 5 6 6 7⑈ ⑈7 7 5 1 2 3 4⑈

Susan B. Anthony   7812
2200 Dollar Drive
Four Bits, Texas 77666   DATE *Feb. 5, 2001*   88-566/223

PAT TO THE
ORDER OF *Amanda Jones* $ | 546.16 |

Five hundred forty-six dollars & 16/100   DOLLARS

Lotsa Money Federal Bank

MEMO _____   *Susan B. Anthony*

⑈1 2 2 3 4 5 6 6 7⑈ ⑈7 7 5 1 2 3 4⑈

Susan B. Anthony   7813
2200 Dollar Drive
Four Bits, Texas 77666   DATE *Feb. 5, 2001*   88-566/223

PAT TO THE
ORDER OF *Leon Letty* $ | 576.49 |

Five hundred seventy-six dollars & 49/100   DOLLARS

Lotsa Money Federal Bank

MEMO _____   *Susan B. Anthony*

⑈1 2 2 3 4 5 6 6 7⑈ ⑈7 7 5 1 2 3 4⑈

Susan B. Anthony
2200 Dollar Drive
Four Bits, Texas 77666

7814

88-566/223

DATE *Feb. 5, 2001*

PAY TO THE
ORDER OF *Paula Peyton* $ | 543.49

Five hundred forty-three dollars & 49/100 DOLLARS

Lotsa Money Federal Bank

MEMO _____ *Susan B. Anthony*

⑈12234566 7⑈ ⑈77 51234⑈

Susan B. Anthony
2200 Dollar Drive
Four Bits, Texas 77666

7815

88-566/223

DATE *Feb. 5, 2001*

PAY TO THE
ORDER OF *Nancy Dawson* $ | 912.43

Nine hundred twelve dollars & 43/100 DOLLARS

Lotsa Money Federal Bank

MEMO _____ *Susan B. Anthony*

⑈12234566 7⑈ ⑈77 51234⑈

Susan B. Anthony
2200 Dollar Drive
Four Bits, Texas 77666

7816

88-566/223

DATE *Feb. 5, 2001*

PAY TO THE
ORDER OF *Pauline Lott* $ | 994.93

Nine hundred ninety-four dollars & 93/100 DOLLARS

Lotsa Money Federal Bank

MEMO _____ *Susan B. Anthony*

⑈12234566 7⑈ ⑈77 51234⑈

Susan B. Anthony   7817
2200 Dollar Drive
Four Bits, Texas 77666   DATE *Feb. 5, 2001* 88-566/223

PAT TO THE
ORDER OF *Rose Deighton* $ | 117.16 |

One hundred seventeen dollars & 16/100 DOLLARS

Lotsa Money Federal Bank

MEMO _____   *Susan B. Anthony*

⑈1 2 2 3 4 5 6 6 7⑈ ⑈77 5 1 2 3 4⑈

Susan B. Anthony   7818
2200 Dollar Drive
Four Bits, Texas 77666   DATE *Feb. 5, 2001* 88-566/223

PAT TO THE
ORDER OF *Candace Smith* $ | 525.63 |

Five hundred twenty-five dollars & 63/100   DOLLARS

Lotsa Money Federal Bank

MEMO _____   *Susan B. Anthony*

⑈1 2 2 3 4 5 6 6 7⑈ ⑈77 5 1 2 3 4⑈

Susan B. Anthony   7819
2200 Dollar Drive
Four Bits, Texas 77666   DATE *Feb. 5, 2001* 88-566/223

PAT TO THE
ORDER OF *Laura Jameson* $ | 449.49 |

Four hundred forty-nine dollars & 49/100   DOLLARS

Lotsa Money Federal Bank

MEMO _____   *Susan B. Anthony*

⑈1 2 2 3 4 5 6 6 7⑈ ⑈77 5 1 2 3 4⑈

Susan B. Anthony
2200 Dollar Drive
Four Bits, Texas 77666

7820

DATE *Feb. 5, 2001* 88-566/223

PAT TO THE
ORDER OF *Kenneth Drew* $ 546.49

Five hundred forty-six dollars & 49/100 DOLLARS

Lotsa Money Federal Bank

MEMO _____ *Susan B. Anthony*

⑆1 2 2 3 4 5 6 6 7⑆ ⑈7 7 5 1 2 3 4⑈

Susan B. Anthony
2200 Dollar Drive
Four Bits, Texas 77666

7821

DATE *Feb. 5, 2001* 88-566/223

PAT TO THE
ORDER OF *Leslie Harper* $ 182.19

One hundred eighty-two dollars & 19/100 DOLLARS

Lotsa Money Federal Bank

MEMO _____ *Susan B. Anthony*

⑆1 2 2 3 4 5 6 6 7⑆ ⑈7 7 5 1 2 3 4⑈

Susan B. Anthony
2200 Dollar Drive
Four Bits, Texas 77666

7822

DATE *Feb. 5, 2001* 88-566/223

PAT TO THE
ORDER OF *Janice Elliott* $ 511.59

Five hundred eleven dollars & 59/100 DOLLARS

Lotsa Money Federal Bank

MEMO _____ *Susan B. Anthony*

⑆1 2 2 3 4 5 6 6 7⑆ ⑈7 7 5 1 2 3 4⑈

Check 7823

Susan B. Anthony
2200 Dollar Drive
Four Bits, Texas 77666

88-566/223

DATE *Feb. 5, 2001*

7823

PAT TO THE ORDER OF *Andrew Mills*

$ 726.16

Seven hundred twenty-six dollars & 16/100 DOLLARS

Lotsa Money Federal Bank

MEMO

Susan B. Anthony

⑆123456673⑆ ⑈77 51234⑈

Check 7824

Susan B. Anthony
2200 Dollar Drive
Four Bits, Texas 77666

88-566/223

DATE *Feb. 5, 2001*

7824

PAT TO THE ORDER OF *Bart Bailey*

$ 517.66

Five hundred seventeen dollars & 66/100 DOLLARS

Lotsa Money Federal Bank

MEMO

Susan B. Anthony

⑆123456673⑆ ⑈77 51234⑈

Check 7825

Susan B. Anthony
2200 Dollar Drive
Four Bits, Texas 77666

88-566/223

DATE *Feb. 5, 2001*

7825

PAT TO THE ORDER OF *Ben Martin*

$ 756.76

Seven hundred fifty-six dollars & 76/100 DOLLARS

Lotsa Money Federal Bank

MEMO

Susan B. Anthony

⑆123456673⑆ ⑈77 51234⑈

Order Test

In this test, the student simulates data entry for a retail ordering system. The computer will generate all data needed for this test. **Figure 13** shows the beginning window for the Order Test.

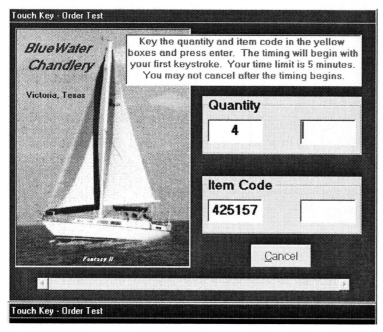

Figure 13

Order Instructions

Read the following set of instructions before beginning the test. The test may be canceled before the timing begins, but not after.

- Similar to Touch Key Lessons and Drills, data to be keyed will appear in two white boxes. You will enter data in the two corresponding yellow boxes.

- Backspace, Shift + Tab, and Tab are functional during this test. It is not possible to move to a previous screen.

- This is a 5-minute test. A scroll bar will appear on the screen to give you an indication of the time remaining. Also, during the last ten seconds of the test, the numbers to be keyed will turn red.

After the test has been completed, Strokes per Hour, Errors, and Percent Accuracy are given. At this point, the test and your actual keystrokes may be printed. Scores may be printed at any time from the Test Log under Print on the Main menu.

Payroll Test

This application is designed to give you experience in keying numerical data using payroll information. You should attempt to key as quickly as possible while maintaining accuracy. A maximum time limit of 10 minutes is given for this job. The timing will stop when you have finished keying the payroll data or when the maximum time limit has been reached—whichever comes first (see **Figure 14**).

Read the following set of instructions before beginning the test. The test may be canceled before the timing begins, but not after.

Payroll Instructions

- Key the payroll information contained in **Table 5** in the appropriate box and press Enter.

- Do not key hyphens in the Social Security numbers.

- Decimals must be keyed when entering amounts for Rates, Regular Hours, and Overtime Hours.

- If there are no overtime hours, press Enter to continue.

- Take care not to lose your place. Records MUST be keyed in the order in which they appear on the form.

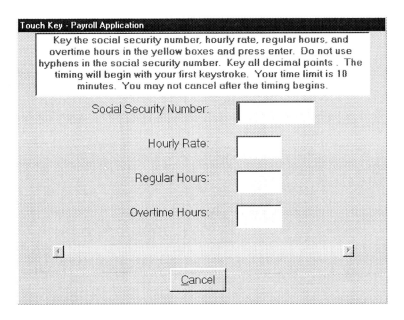

Figure 14

- It is possible to correct information on the current screen in the current box by using Backspace. To move to a previous box, press Shift + Tab (hold down the Shift key and press the Tab key). To move to the next box, press TAB. However, remember that the time clock is running.

- It is not possible to move to a previous screen.

After the test has been completed, Strokes per Hour, Errors, and Percent Accuracy will appear. At this point the application may be printed. Scores may be printed at any time from the Test Log on the Print menu.

Use the following payroll information to complete the payroll test.

Blue Water Chandlery, Victoria, TX
Payroll Register
For Pay Period Dec. 18, 2003 to Dec. 25, 2003

Emp. #	SS #	Reg. Rate	Reg. Hours	O.T. Hours
001	977766775	12.50	40.00	
002	828144362	12.75	40.00	5.50
003	819634856	7.50	32.00	
004	660459234	7.50	40.00	
005	578215591	15.25	40.00	
006	329371954	12.50	40.00	
007	958552951	12.50	40.00	8.00
008	596594592	12.50	32.00	
009	852923343	12.50	40.00	
010	439255221	12.75	38.00	
011	449771214	12.75	40.00	6.50
012	563794514	15.00	40.00	
013	485274747	15.05	40.00	
014	292543323	7.50	40.00	4.00
015	721536363	7.50	24.00	
016	855923443	12.50	40.00	8.50
017	696548211	12.50	40.00	8.00

018	392919155	7.50	40.00	4.00
019	879476654	11.00	40.00	8.00
020	439753226	8.50	40.00	
021	229664391	25.00	40.00	
022	957196825	7.50	40.00	9.50
023	234274791	8.75	40.00	8.00
024	559642287	9.05	40.00	
025	862575123	12.25	40.00	
026	621923161	9.75	40.00	5.75
027	551852891	10.25	40.00	4.50
028	459771888	12.50	32.00	
029	468212752	12.50	36.00	
030	793928585	8.00	40.00	
031	820583663	9.35	36.00	
032	309594774	12.50	40.00	
033	399600201	11.50	38.00	
034	484180491	7.50	40.00	4.00
035	885272333	7.50	40.00	
036	785533938	8.50	40.00	
037	435388822	7.75	40.00	4.50
038	413535577	9.25	32.00	
039	536114714	10.50	40.00	
040	262723669	7.55	40.00	8.50

Table 5

Invoice Test

In this job, you are to enter data by customer number for invoicing. You must use care in entering the required data on the computer because the screen format is slightly different from that of the paper copy (see **Figure 15**).

Read the following set of instructions before beginning the test. The test may be canceled before the timing begins, but not after.

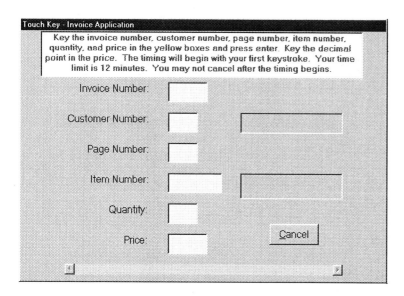

Figure 15

Invoice Instructions

- The Invoice Number and Customer Number MUST be keyed along with each line item.

- Some information will appear automatically. When the customer number is entered, the customer name appears. When the item number is keyed, the nomenclature appears.

- Decimals MUST be keyed.

- Take care not to lose your place.

Hint: Keep your place with your left index finger on the line item while keying with the right hand. Then, when your eyes look elsewhere on the page to see the Invoice Number and Customer Number, you will be able to shift your eyes back to the next line item. This is essential, as the items are not numbered.

- Backspace, Shift + Tab, and Tab are functional in this test. It is not possible to return to a previous screen, however.

- The maximum time limit for this application is 12 minutes. The timing will end when all data has been keyed or when the time limit has been reached—whichever comes first.

When the test has been completed, Strokes per Hour, Errors, and Percent Accuracy will appear. At this point the test and actual student keystrokes may be printed. The scores may be printed at any time from the Test Log under Print on the Main menu.

Turn to the next page to begin the invoice test.

Crafter's Dreamland

1500 Bayou Way, Victoria, TX 77901
1-800-CRAFTER   Fax: 1-361-771-6464

INVOICE 92001

CUSTOMER No.   860

November 1, 2003

Sold to: Jessica Long
213 Waco St.
Nashville, TN 53333

PAGE NO.	ITEM NO.	QUANTITY	DESCRIPTION	PRICE
209	100639	5	Peter Rabbit Quilt Panel Kit	19.99
420	900767	3	Willows Fabric Yardage	7.50
420	100508	10	Willows Fat Quarter Packet	10.99
209	100640	5	Peter Rabbit Fat Quarter Packet	11.99
20	100463	1	Flowers, Flowers Pattern	8.00
21	100513	5	Birdhouse Pattern	8.00

Crafter's Dreamland

INVOICE 92002

1500 Bayou Way, Victoria, TX 77901

CUSTOMER No.   310

1-800-CRAFTER   Fax: 1-361-771-6464

November 1, 2003

Sold to: Natalie Waits
634 N. Lakeview
Coronado, CA 88888

PAGE NO.	ITEM NO.	QUANTITY	DESCRIPTION	PRICE
22	100747	1	Tulip Pattern	4.95
420	900767	6	Willows Fabric Yardage	7.50
420	100508	1	Willows Fat Quarter Packet	10.99
33	100559	3	Quilter's Vest	31.99
430	621251	2	1 3/4" Quilt Pins	2.95
430	621256	3	1 3/8" Red Glass-Head Silk Pins	4.98

Crafter's Dreamland

1500 Bayou Way, Victoria, TX 77901
1-800-CRAFTER   Fax: 1-361-771-6464

INVOICE 92003
CUSTOMER No.   949
November 1, 2003

Sold to: Mrs. Juan Velasquez
             2000 Alamo Dr.
             San Antonio, TX 75000

PAGE NO.	ITEM NO.	QUANTITY	DESCRIPTION	PRICE
33	100559	1	Quilter's Vest	31.99
13	631334	2	Transparent Thread	4.25
13	631577	1	Metalic Thread Assortment	34.90
209	100640	1	Peter Rabbit Fat Quarter Packet	11.99
20	100463	3	Flowers, Flowers Pattern	8.00
26	122651	1	Polyester Thread	9.57

Crafter's Dreamland

INVOICE 92004

1500 Bayou Way, Victoria, TX 77901

CUSTOMER No.   329

1-800-CRAFTER   Fax: 1-361-771-6464

November 1, 2003

Sold to: Jennifer Dupree
1000 Circle Blvd.
Atlanta, GA 80000

PAGE NO.	ITEM NO.	QUANTITY	DESCRIPTION	PRICE
420	100508	1	Willows Fat Quarter Packet	10.99
22	100747	6	Tulip Pattern	4.95
209	100640	14	Peter Rabbit Fat Quarter Packet	11.99
33	100559	3	Quilter's Vest	31.99
52	100188	2	Machine Quilting w/Decorative Threads	21.95
430	621256	3	1 3/8" Red Glass-Head Silk Pins	4.98

Crafter's Dreamland

INVOICE **92005**

1500 Bayou Way, Victoria, TX 77901

CUSTOMER No.   200

1-800-CRAFTER   Fax: 1-361-771-6464

November 1, 2003

Sold to: Robert Ainsley
P. O. Box 91202
Vicksburg, TN 52333

PAGE NO.	ITEM NO.	QUANTITY	DESCRIPTION	PRICE
53	223785	5	Holidays on Parade	15.95
22	100747	6	Tulip Pattern	4.95
209	100640	5	Peter Rabbit Fat Quarter Packet	11.99
54	100162	5	Creative Cotton Chenille	16.99
52	100188	2	Machine Quilting w/Decorative Threads	21.95
43	621672	36	Thread Heaven	2.80

Crafter's Dreamland

1500 Bayou Way, Victoria, TX 77901
1-800-CRAFTER   Fax: 1-361-771-6464

INVOICE **92006**

CUSTOMER No.   551
November 1, 2003

Sold to: Lacey Anderson Design Shop
            8300 Santa Fe Dr., #222
            Albuquerque, NM 55544

PAGE NO.	ITEM NO.	QUANTITY	DESCRIPTION	PRICE
424	100503	10	10" Squares Packet	41.99
13	631577	12	Metalic Thread Assortment	34.90
209	100640	12	Peter Rabbit Fat Quarter Packet	11.99
33	100559	6	Quilter's Vest	31.99
21	100513	15	Birdhouse Pattern	8.00
209	100639	12	Peter Rabbit Quilt Panel Kit	19.99

Crafter's Dreamland

1500 Bayou Way, Victoria, TX 77901
1-800-CRAFTER   Fax: 1-361-771-6464

Sold to: Ms. Julie Newman
232 W. Grove St.
New York, NY 10000

INVOICE 92007
CUSTOMER No.   121
November 1, 2003

PAGE NO.	ITEM NO.	QUANTITY	DESCRIPTION	PRICE
33	100559	1	Quilter's Vest	31.99
213	100534	1	House to House Pattern	8.25
224	900905	1	Natures Textures Fat 1/4 Packet	14.90
209	100640	1	Peter Rabbit Fat Quarter Packet	11.99
20	100463	1	Flowers, Flowers Pattern	8.00
22	100747	1	Tulip Pattern	4.95

Counting Errors

Each of the following is counted as one error by the Touch Key software.

Incorrect keystroke
Missing keystroke
Incorrect place value

Desktop
Calculator

PART 2

APPLYING YOUR
TEN-KEY SKILL

Using the Desktop Calculator

Lesson 1 – The Desktop Calculator

A typical keyboard of a desktop calculator is shown in **Figure 16**. Each marked key is identified and described in **Table 6**.

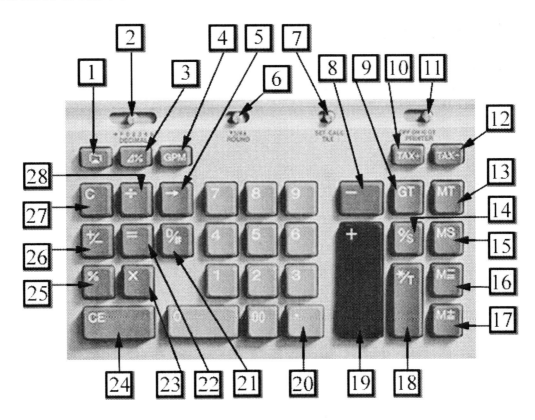

Figure 16 Keyboard of TI 5660® Desktop Calculator

	Symbol	Name	Description
		Identification & Description of Desktop Calculator Keys	
	Symbol	Name	Description
1	↑	Paper Feed	Advances the paper tape
2	DECIMAL	Decimal Selector	+ —allows addition and subtraction of numbers without entering the decimal point. (The decimal point is automatically placed at 2 places in any number entered.) F— the number of decimal places varies based on the result 0 2 3 4 6— sets the number of decimal places at 1, 2, 3, 4, or 6
3	Δ%	Percent Change	Computes percent of increase/decrease
4	GPM	Gross Profit Margin	Calculates selling price and profit or loss on an item
5	→	Correction	Removes the last digit entered in the display
6	ROUND	Rounding Switch	Sets the type of rounding: down, 5/4, or up

	Symbol	Name	Description
		Identification & Description of Desktop Calculator Keys	
7	TAX	Tax Switch	a) SET—sets tax rate to perform tax calculations b) CALC—stores the tax rate
8	–	Subtraction	Subtracts the number from value in display
9	GT	Grand Total	Displays and prints the grand total of all totals
10	TAX+	Tax Plus	Adds stored tax rate to value in display
11	PRINTER	Printer Switch	a) OFF, calculations are displayed but not printed b) ON, Calculations are displayed and printed c) IC, both printer and item counter are active. Press */T or MT key to clear item counter. d) GT, accumulates a running grand total of all calculations. Press GT key to print a grand total. Press GT key again to clear the grand total.
12	TAX–	Tax Minus	Subtracts stored tax rate from value in display
13	MT	Memory Total	Displays and prints value in memory, clears the memory, and resets item counter to zero
14	◊/S	Subtotal	Displays and prints total, but does not clear the total
15	MS	Memory Subtotal	Displays and prints total in memory, but does not clear memory
16	M– =	Memory Minus	Subtracts displayed value from memory. If a multiplication or division operation is pending, M – = completes it and subtracts the result from memory.
17	M+ =	Memory Plus	Adds displayed value to memory. If a multiplication or division operation is pending, M + = completes it and adds the result to memory.
18	*/T	Total	Displays and prints the total, clears the total, and resets the item counter to zero.
19	+	Addition	Adds the number to value in display.
20	.	Decimal	Enters a decimal
21	D/#	Date/Number	Prints a date or reference number without affecting calculations
22	=	Equals key	Displays products and quotients
23	×	Multiplication	Sets the machine up to multiply the value in the display by the next number entered.
24	CE	Clear Entry	Clears an entry, error, or overflow
25	%	Percent	Interprets the number in display as a percentage
26	+/–	Reverse	Reverses the sign (+ or -) of the displayed number
27	C	Clear	Clears entire pending operation except memory or grand total
28	÷	Division	Prepares the machine to divide the value in the display by the next number entered.

Table 6

10-Key Touch Key

Organization of Workspace

Position the desktop calculator slightly to the right of your body (**Figure 17**).

Sit with your feet flat on the floor. Lean forward slightly. Your arm should hang comfortably at your side from shoulder to elbow. Raise your right hand, curl your fingers, and poise them over the keypad.

Figure 17 Posture

When keying from paper copy, place the paper copy so that you can keep your place using the left hand.

Figure 18 Keeping Your Place

Lesson 2 – Addition

Keystroking Technique – Home Row Keys

Home Row. The 4, 5, and 6 keys are the home row keys on the key pad. Curl the fingers of the right hand. Place the index finger on the 4 key, the middle finger on the 5 key, and the ring finger on the 6 key (**Figure 19**). The 5 key usually has a small raised dot or bar on its surface to help you identify it by touch.

Similar to using the numberpad on a computer, the fingers should be in position to strike the home row keys with a straight downward motion. The wrist should be straight, not angled, or bent.

Addition on Desktop Calculators

Figure 19 The 4, 5, 6 Keys

The order of entry for a typical addition problem on the desktop calculator involves keying each of the addends followed by the plus key. Press the total key to print the sum on the paper tape (if using the print function), reset the item counter, end the problem, and clear the machine for the next problem. (The sum will still be shown in the display, but the machine's register is ready for the next problem.)

Figure 19 The 4, 5, 6 Keys

Keystroking Technique – Addition

With the index, middle, and ring fingers in position over the 4, 5, and 6 keys (the home row), use the little finger to press the addition key (**Figure 20**) and the total key (**Figure 21**). Attempt to press the keys without moving the home row fingers from their positions over the home row keys.

Figure 20 Addition Key

Correcting Keying Errors

Certain keystrokes may be corrected on the desktop calculator using the following techniques:

Figure 21 Total Key

1. To clear an incorrect number that has been keyed, press the clear entry (CE) key before pressing an operation key.

2. To clear the last digit from the display, press the backspace (→) key before pressing an arithmetic operation key or the total key.

3. To cancel an addition or subtraction operation, press the opposite operation key.

4. To undo an incorrect number that has been added, subtract the same number.

5. To undo an incorrect number that has been subtracted, add the same number.

6. To cancel an addition to memory or subtraction from memory operation, press the opposite memory operation key.

Machine Setup

1. Set the decimal selector on F or 0. Set the rounding switch on 5/4.

2. Set the tax switch on CALC.

3. Set the printer switch on IC (item counter). With the printer switch set on IC, the number of items entered for each problem will be *counted and printed on the paper tape* when the total key is pressed.

Note: Although a paper tape is not necessary to complete problems, a paper tape is often used in business for verification of totals. A paper tape is necessary if you wish to count entries for each problem.

4. Key the numbers and symbols in the order shown in the procedure. The answer in the box should match the answer in the calculator display.

Problem:	Procedure:	Check:
47	47 +	54 +
46	46 +	46 +
+54	54 + */T	47 + */T
	147	147

Addition Practice Problems – Keys 4 through 6

Key the following addition problems, using the plus (+) key after each addend and the total key (*/T) to find the sum. *Remember that it is not necessary to clear the display after pressing the total key.* Compare your answers with the ones given. The paper tape should indicate that 10 entries were made for each problem.

1.		2.		3.		4.		5.		6.		7.		8.	
	44		45		54		56		44		65		66		64
	54		55		56		65		46		55		65		65
	46		56		64		64		45		54		46		55
	46		54		65		66		45		54		64		54
	44		55		55		64		44		56		66		44
	45		54		64		65		44		55		65		46
	46		54		66		66		46		66		66		46
	54		54		64		46		65		64		64		66
	45		56		65		44		66		46		65		55
	64		66		66		45		64		56		56		55
	488		549		619		581		509		571		623		550

Keystroking Technique – Top Row

Top Row. Strike the upper row keys with the pad or fleshy part of the finger (see **Figure 22**).

Figure 22 The 7 Key

After striking a key on the top row, return your finger to the appropriate key on the home row. The 4 (or index) finger reaches upward to strike the 7 key, the 5 (or middle) finger strikes the 8 key, and the 6 (or ring) finger strikes the 9 key.

Machine Setup
Set the decimal selector on F or 0.
Set the rounding switch on 5/4.
Set the tax switch on CALC.
Set the printer switch on IC (item counter).

Addition Practice Problems – Keys 4 through 9

Key the following addition problems, using the plus (+) key after each addend and the total key (*/T) to find the sum. *Remember that it is not necessary to clear the display after pressing the total key.* Compare your answers with the ones given.

1.		2.		3.		4.		5.		6.		7.		8.	
	64		55		84		96		54		95		46		74
	54		55		67		65		46		58		99		79
	47		56		74		64		45		57		56		85
	46		88		75		86		58		44		67		87
	48		57		57		67		47		86		68		74
	69		59		78		68		44		55		65		79
	84		94		89		69		99		96		66		76
	94		84		97		76		95		67		74		96
	45		87		79		74		96		46		69		48
	64		86		76		75		97		56		97		85
	615		721		776		740		681		660		707		783

Score (Correct Answers ÷ No. of Assigned Problems) _____

Lesson 2 Exercises

Exercise 1

Add and check. Two blanks are provided; one for the first answer and one for the check answer.

4	8	7	6	88	4	9
5	6	6	7	4	9	77
6	9	5	56	5	5	5
+55	+7	+4	+9	+6	+6	+6

1. _____ 2. _____ 3. _____ 4. _____ 5. _____ 6. _____ 7. _____

Add and check. Remember to use commas in answers when necessary.

589	858	69	74	44	696	474
47	47	56	54	56	58	99
45	68	474	45	77	47	69
+875	+57	+66	+69	+659	+69	+565

8. _____ 9. _____ 10. _____ 11. _____ 12. _____ 13. _____ 14. _____

Add and check.

99 + 696 + 55 = _____   47 + 55+ 796 = _____   77 + 8 + 746 = _____
        15. _____   16. _____   17. _____

74 + 744 + 65 = _____   48 + 85+ 578 = _____   66 + 9 + 769 = _____
        18. _____   19. _____   20. _____

Exercise 2

Strokes Per Minute Score _____

Accuracy Score (Correct Strokes ÷ Total Strokes) _____

1-Minute Addition Timing (Keys 4 through 9)

Complete as many of the problems as possible in one minute by adding. Work quickly and accurately. The numbers in parentheses indicate the cumulative number of strokes for problems attempted. For example, if you complete problems 1 through 5 in one minute, your strokes-per-minute score is 155. *Optional*: Instructions for longer timings follow this timing.

1.	44	2.	45	3.	54	4.	56	5.	44	6.	65	7.	66	8.	64
	54		55		57		65		46		58		69		69
	47		56		74		64		45		57		46		85
	46		58		75		66		48		54		67		87
	48		57		87		67		47		56		68		74
	49		59		78		68		44		55		65		79
	84		54		89		69		49		66		66		76
	94		84		97		76		95		67		64		96
	45		87		79		74		96		46		69		88
	64		86		76		75		97		56		96		85
31)		62)		93)		124)		155)		186)		217)		248)

9.	10.	11.	12.	13.	14.	15.	16.
74	47	45	65	66	77	76	84
49	84	75	46	86	74	79	58
84	94	58	58	76	75	67	86
85	47	95	59	96	76	47	48
47	46	98	57	56	78	75	78
48	48	96	45	46	79	78	89
45	49	65	58	69	97	79	85
44	45	55	59	67	67	87	87
46	44	57	57	68	57	74	84
94	64	75	56	66	47	77	86
279)	310)	341)	372)	403)	434)	465)	496)

17.	18.	19.	20.	21.	22.	23.	24.
94	85	74	76	84	65	99	86
96	88	84	78	87	86	49	88
95	84	94	47	95	69	65	58
68	86	57	49	94	76	79	85
89	87	57	95	99	46	58	78
84	89	58	69	85	54	98	48
57	95	59	96	76	58	57	85
59	96	55	76	64	68	97	86
69	76	56	77	95	76	75	89
67	74	64	87	55	86	76	87
527)	558)	589)	620)	651)	682)	713)	744)

25.	26.	27.	28.	29.	30.	31.	32.
44	58	67	96	95	89	76	64
84	56	46	99	97	59	85	69
96	89	56	59	67	58	76	68
95	86	87	89	98	68	74	67
85	57	89	69	69	67	79	46
76	48	88	67	76	57	98	65
74	89	84	69	48	94	97	86
57	68	85	68	87	68	96	85
59	58	59	64	89	86	59	89
56	57	65	69	86	69	64	96
775)	806)	837)	868)	899)	930)	961)	992)

If you wish to take longer timings, divide your total strokes by the number of minutes in the timing. For example, if you take a 3-minute timing, divide your total strokes by 3 to get your *strokes per minute* score.

To calculate your *percent of accuracy* score, use the following method.

Using the calculator tape, check each keystroke. For incomplete problems, count each number and each operation key as one stroke and add to the total strokes indicated beside the previous problem. Subtract incorrect strokes from total strokes to find total correct strokes. Divide correct strokes by total strokes. Convert to a percent. This is your *percent of accuracy* score.

Example: 190 total strokes, 178 correct strokes
178 correct strokes divided by 190 total strokes =.94 (rounded).
Convert to a decimal number. 94% is your *percent of accuracy* score.

Some instructors may prefer to use total problem accuracy when calculating a grade. To use this method, check <u>answers only</u> for all completed problems. Divide the number of correct problems by the number of problems attempted. This will give you the percent of problem accuracy.

Example: 6 problems were attempted, 5 were correct.
5 divided by 6 =.8333 or 83% problem accuracy

Or, you may add together keystrokes for problems with correct answers only. (In this exercise, there are 31 strokes in each problem.) Divide the number of correct problem keystrokes by the total keystrokes for all problems attempted.

Example: 6 problems were attempted, 5 were correct.
5 x 31 = 155
155 keystrokes divided by 186 keystrokes =.8333 or 83%

Lesson 2 Answers to Selected Problems

Exercise 1
  1. 70 3. 22 5. 103 7. 97 9. 1,030 11. 242 13. 870 15. 850 17. 831 19. 711

Exercise 2
  1. 575 3. 766 5. 611 7. 676 9. 616 11. 719 13. 696 15. 739 17. 778 19. 658 21. 834 23. 753
  25. 726 27. 726 29. 812 31. 804

Lesson 3 – Subtraction

Keystroking Technique – Bottom Row

Bottom Row. Strike the keys on the bottom row with the fingernail portion of the fingertips, and then return the finger to the home row. Strike the 1 key with the 4 finger, strike the 2 key with the 5 finger, and strike the 3 key with the 6 finger (**Figure 23**).

Zero and Decimal Keys. Strike the single 0 key with the thumb and the decimal key with the ring finger.

Figure 23 The 3 Key

Subtraction

The order of entry for a typical subtraction problem on the desktop calculator involves first keying the minuend followed by the plus key, then keying the subtrahend followed by the minus and total keys. On a desktop with a two-color ribbon, the items subtracted and any negative differences will print in red.

Checking the problem: With the difference still displayed, press the plus key, and then add the subtrahend. The difference should equal the minuend of the original problem.

Keystroking Technique – Subtraction

With the index, middle, and ring fingers in position over the 4, 5, and 6 keys, use the little finger to press the subtraction key (**Figure 24**). Attempt to press the key without moving the home row fingers from the correct position over the home row keys.

Machine Setup

Set the decimal selector on F or 0. Set the rounding switch on 5/4. Set the printer switch on IC (item counter). The Total key is shown in a box for clarity.

Figure 24 Subtraction Key

Problem:	Procedure:	Check:
47	47 +	31 +
-16	16 − */T	16 + */T
	31	47

Subtraction Practice Problems Using Keys 1 through 9

Set the decimal selector on F. Key the following subtraction problems, using the plus key after each positive number, the subtraction key after each negative number, and the total key to find the answer. Compare your answer with the one given.

1,164	2,155	8,184	3,496	8,104	2,390.5	7,146	9,674
-24.5	-52.05	-64.11	-30	-240	-58.07	-309	-270
-17.3	-53	-71	-104	-340	-507	-56	-3.85
-16	-82.03	-72.06	-22.6	-1,580	-14.04	-60	-18.07
-18	-51	-51	-3.07	-240	-806	-62.50	-10.71
-39.6	-53	-702	-26.08	-540	-25.5	-65	-373
-24	-91	-83	-306	-190	-96	-63.09	-173
-34	-81.06	-91	-1.16	-190	-367	-174	-30.93
-15	-82	-703	-2.24	-290	-46	-69.02	-10.42
-64.2	-83	-73	-105	-390	-256	-37	-28.02

1. 911.4	2. 1,526.86	3. 6,273.83	4. 2,895.85	5. 4,104	6. 214.89	7. 6,250.39	8. 8,756

Lesson 3 Exercises

Exercise 1

Subtract. Check by adding. The first problem has been completed for you.

95	38	76	91	27	922
-16	-25	-64	-59	-19	-71

1. __79__ 2. _____ 3. _____ 4. _____ 5. _____ 6. _____
   +16
   __95__

Subtract and check. Remember to use commas in answers when necessary.

28	331	46	627	5,228
-11	-34	-24	-124	-156

7. _____ 8. _____ 9. _____ 10. _____ 11. _____

Subtract and check.

12. 4,132 - 551 = _____   _____   13. 2,291 − 1,144 = _____   _____

Exercise 2

1-Minute Addition Timing (Keys 1 through 9)

1.	34	2.	41	3.	24	4.	26	5.	14	6.	62	7.	36	8.	61
	52		55		27		62		16		28		39		63
	47		53		74		61		15		27		16		82
	16		58		78		63		18		24		37		81
	28		57		57		64		17		26		38		44
	25		59		75		65		14		25		35		43
	41		51		59		63		19		33		33		16
	21		81		91		79		35		37		34		36
	52		87		73		71		36		16		31		82
	58		83		73		72		37		26		32		25
31)		62)		93)		124)		155)		186)		217)		248)

9.	74	10.	47	11.	45	12.	65	13.	66	14.	77	15.	76	16.	84
	49		84		75		46		86		74		79		58
	84		94		58		58		76		75		67		86
	85		47		95		59		96		76		47		48
	47		46		98		57		56		78		75		78
	48		48		96		45		46		79		78		89
	45		49		65		58		69		97		79		85
	44		45		55		59		67		67		87		87
	46		44		57		57		68		57		74		84
	94		64		75		56		66		47		77		86
279)		310)		341)		372)		403)		434)		465)		496)

17.		18.		19.		20.		21.		22.		23.		24.	
	64		82		71		76		24		32		79		86
	66		88		84		78		27		36		49		82
	65		84		94		47		35		13		65		52
	38		86		57		49		34		32		79		85
	29		87		57		95		39		13		52		72
	24		89		58		69		25		31		92		42
	87		95		59		96		16		58		57		85
	89		96		55		76		34		38		97		83
	39		76		56		77		25		16		75		89
	37		74		64		87		21		56		73		81
527)		558)		589)		620)		651)		682)		713)		744)

Lesson 3 Answers to Selected Problems

Exercise 1
1. 79 3. 12 5. 8 7. 17 9. 22 11. 5,072 13. 1,147

Exercise 2
1. 374 3. 631 5. 221 7. 331 9. 616 11. 719 13. 696 15. 739 17. 538 19. 655 21. 280 23. 718

Lesson 4 – Multiplication and Multifactor Multiplication

Keystroking Technique – Holding a Pencil

Refer to **Figure 25** for the correct method of holding a pencil while keying numbers. The pencil is held between the thumb and the first joint of the index finger. The point of the pencil should extend slightly past the first joint of the little finger. The pencil may be switched to a position for writing simply by moving the thumb to the left. This shifts the pencil to an upright position and allows the fingers and thumb to move to the normal position used in writing. The reverse of these movements will place the pencil back in the position that allows for the keying of numbers.

Note: If you write with your left hand, there is no need for you to hold a pencil in your right hand while keying. Simply record answers as you normally would while keying numbers with your right hand.

Figure 25

Add the following problems while holding a pencil. As you complete each problem, write your answer below the problem. After you have completed all the problems, check your answers with those given.

1.	2.	3.	4.	5.	6.	7.	8.
64	55	84	96	54	95	46	74
24	52	64	35	46	58	99	79
17	53	71	64	45	57	56	85
16	82	72	26	58	44	61	87
18	51	51	37	47	86	62	71
39	53	72	68	44	55	65	73
24	91	83	36	99	96	63	73
34	81	91	16	95	67	74	93
15	82	73	24	96	46	69	42
64	83	73	35	97	56	37	82
315	683	734	437	681	660	632	759

Keystroking Technique – Equals and Multiplication Key

On the desktop calculator, the equals key (=) is used to find the product of a multiplication problem, not the total key. If located to the left of the keyboard, the equals key and the multiplication key (x) are both pressed with the index finger. While reaching for the equals or multiplication key, try to leave the ring finger anchored on the 6 key. After keying the equals or multiplication key, bring the index finger back to the 4 key. Feel for the raised bar or dot on the 5 key to make sure fingers are in correct position on the home row before continuing to key numbers. Check with your instructor if the equals and total keys are located elsewhere on the keyboard. Note that although it is not necessary to use the multiplication and equals keys strictly by touch, it is important to use correct fingering, which will help you become more efficient. Productive employees are valuable employees!

The order of entry for a typical multiplication problem on the desktop calculator involves first keying the multiplicand followed by the multiplication key, then keying the multiplier followed by the equals key. To check the problem, reverse the multiplicand and multiplier. Solve again. The two products should match.

Problem:	Procedure:	Check:
42	42 x	12 x
x 12	12 =	42 =
	504	504

Multifactor Multiplication

Problems containing more than two factors may be easily solved. Key the factors and signs as shown below for a problem containing four factors. Operation keys to be pressed and the answer are shown in boxes.

55 x 42 x 3 x 11 = 76,230

Lesson 4 Exercises

Exercise 1

Multiply and check.

95	38	76	91	27	922	52
x 16	x 25	x 64	x 59	x 19	x 71	x 28

1._____ 2. _____ 3. _____ 4. _____ 5. _____ 6. _____ 7. _____

Multiply and check.

28	331	46	627	5,228	8,352	7,436
x 11	x 34	x 24	x 124	x 156	x 936	x 652

8. _____ 9. _____10. _____11. _____12. _____13. _____14. _____

Multiply and check.

15. 4,132 x 551 = _____   16. 2,291 x 144 = _____
17. 4,225 x 363 = _____   18. 3,916 x 136 = _____
19. 413 x 514 = _____   20. 3,463 x 1,385 = _____
21. 53,462 x 139 = _____   22. 72,221 x 258 = _____

Exercise 2

Multifactor Multiplication
23. 13 x 112 x 12 = _____   24. 2, 455 x 12 x 9 = _____
25. 312 x 98 x 120 = _____   26. 2,557 x 36 x 22 = _____

Exercise 3

1-Minute Addition Timing (Keys 1 through 6)

1.	64	2.	11	3.	54	4.	26	5.	14	6.	32	7.	36	8.	41
	52		65		51		32		16		25		63		33
	14		23		14		61		15		21		16		52
	16		26		16		33		12		24		31		61
	55		25		24		34		13		26		32		64
	25		12		15		45		14		25		25		13
	41		41		23		43		16		33		33		16
	51		51		31		13		35		34		54		36
	52		54		43		21		36		16		61		52
	25		53		23		12		31		26		52		55
31)		62)		93)		124)		155)		186)		217)		248)	

9.	14	10.	23	11.	15	12.	35	13.	36	14.	22	15.	16	16.	54
	43		24		45		16		56		34		13		26
	64		34		52		24		36		65		64		46
	45		42		15		54		26		36		14		42
	16		16		32		21		56		35		45		62
	13		43		36		45		46		31		23		63
	15		46		65		36		32		41		13		65

10-Key Touch Key

279)	310)	341)	372)	403)	434)	465)	496)
14	15	25	53	13	62	53	67
16	44	51	21	52	54	24	64
64	34	45	16	16	14	11	46

	17.	18.	19.	20.	21.	22.	23.	24.
	34	52	61	36	34	12	13	16
	66	22	64	45	21	26	23	22
	65	54	34	41	15	33	35	32
	32	26	21	53	64	42	63	45
	26	27	51	65	53	53	52	52
	24	46	31	16	45	61	32	62
	51	65	51	26	46	56	55	15
	23	63	55	36	54	22	21	23
	36	56	35	44	25	36	15	33
	34	34	64	21	21	56	43	11
	527)	558)	589)	620)	651)	682)	713)	744)

	25.	26.	27.	28.	29.	30.	31.	32.
	44	22	61	36	25	23	16	34
	41	16	45	63	31	26	25	66
	56	63	53	23	43	32	16	32
	65	46	14	53	12	55	14	61
	55	51	26	63	51	41	13	43
	56	62	32	61	26	11	32	65
	64	13	61	63	32	54	31	53
	51	25	62	35	13	56	36	25
	43	22	53	34	56	53	26	56
	66	31	62	31	46	66	34	36
	775)	806)	837)	868)	899)	930)	961)	992)

Lesson 4 Answers to Selected Problems

Exercise 1
1. 1,520 3. 4,864 5. 513 7. 1,456 9. 11,254 11. 77,748 13. 7,817,472 15. 2,276,732 17. 1,533,675 19. 212,282 21. 7,431,218

Exercise 2
23. 17,472 25. 3,669,120

Exercise 3
1. 395 3. 294 5. 202 7. 403 9. 304 11. 381 13. 369 15. 276 17. 391 19. 467 21. 378 23. 352 25. 541 27. 469 29. 335 31. 243

Lesson 5 – Division and Multifactor Division

Keystroking Technique – 00 Key

Use the middle finger to key the double zero (00) key. Try to keep the little finger hovering over the plus key as you reach for the 00 key. After pressing the 00 key, return fingers to the home row. For numbers containing three zeros, develop the habit of keying the zero key first (with the thumb), then the double zero key (with the middle finger).

Add. Use the double zero key whenever possible. Check your answers.

1.		2.		3.		4.		5.		6.		7.		8.	
	9,064		4,801		7,000		2,700		1,700		3,002		3,009		7,100
	5,002		9,000		8,400		3,200		1,800		2,005		9,003		3,300
	1,804		2,003		9,004		9,100		1,800		2,001		1,900		8,200
	7,006		2,700		7,001		3,300		1,002		2,004		3,001		9,100
	5,500		9,005		2,900		3,700		1,003		2,006		3,002		6,400
	8,005		1,000		7,005		7,800		1,700		2,500		2,005		1,300
	4,190		8,004		2,003		7,300		1,900		3,300		3,003		4,600
	5,100		9,001		3,900		1,003		3,005		3,100		5,007		6,600
	5,000		5,700		7,300		2,000		3,006		1,900		6,001		5,200
	7,700		5,500		2,300		1,200		3,001		2,009		5,200		5,500
	58,371		62,714		56,813		41,303		19,917		23,827		41,131		57,300

Keystroking Technique – Division

Use the index finger to key the division key if it is located to the left of your keyboard. As you reach for the division key, try to keep the ring finger anchored to the six key so that you can easily return your fingers to the home row after pressing the division key. It is not necessary to use the division key by touch only; however, correct fingering is still important.

Division

The order of entry for a typical division problem on the desktop calculator involves first keying the dividend followed by the division key, then keying the divisor followed by the equals key. To check the problem, multiply the quotient by the divisor. The result should match the dividend in the original problem.

Problem:	Procedure:	Check:
5,500 ÷ 11	5,500 ÷	500 x
	11 =	11 =
	500	5,500

Multifactor Division

Problems containing more than one divisor are easily solved on a calculator. Key the dividend followed by the division key, the first divisor followed by the division key, the second divisor followed by the division key and so forth. After keying the last divisor press the equal key. It is important that the order of the dividend and divisors not be changed.

Example: Headquarters for a chain discount store confirmed that their order for 9,000 Brand A televisions would be shipped in two weeks. Management decided to divide them equally among 500 retail territories. Three outlet stores are located within territory WTX. How many Brand A televisions will each store in territory WTX receive?

$$9000 \div 500 \div 3 = \boxed{6}$$

Name _____

Class/Section _____

Score (Correct Answers + No. of Assigned Problems) _____

Lesson 5 Exercises

Exercise 1

Divide and check.

1. $91 \div 13 =$ _____
2. $816 \div 8 =$ _____
3. $273 \div 3 =$ _____
4. $266 \div 7 =$ _____
5. $522 \div 18 =$ _____
6. $267 \div 3 =$ _____
7. $364 \div 7 =$ _____
8. $705 \div 15 =$ _____
9. $440 \div 8 =$ _____
10. $975 \div 25 =$ _____
11. $2,288 \div 26 =$ _____
12. $1,216 \div 8 =$ _____
13. $2,925 \div 45 =$ _____
14. $2,232 \div 62 =$ _____
15. $1,593 \div 27 =$ _____
16. $2,646 \div 98 =$ _____
17. $1,254 \div 33 =$ _____
18. $1,845 \div 15 =$ _____

Multifactor Division

19. $5,600 \div 700 \div 2 =$ _____
20. $10,800 \div 120 \div 9 =$ _____
21. $8,976 \div 34 \div 33 =$ _____
22. $5,040 \div 4 \div 84 =$ _____

Strokes Per Minute Score _____

Accuracy Score (Correct Strokes + Total Strokes) _____

Exercise 2

Comprehensive Speed and Accuracy.

1-Minute Addition Timing (Keys 1 through 9, 0, 00, minus, and decimal keys)

	1.	2.	3.	4.	5.	6.	7.	8.
	55	15	58	28	36	32	36	71
	47	65	52	27	56	38	63	83
	69	25	59	21	53	53	37	92
	58	26	96	55	52	24	38	41
	54	35	57	52	33	26	32	54
	56	12	51	23	13	25	25	63
	51	41	54	29	15	33	33	16
	51	67	53	51	35	34	34	26
	52	64	25	21	36	39	61	32
	53	53	23	12	37	37	57	55
31)		62)	93)	124)	155)	186)	217)	248)

	9.	10.	11.	12.	13.	14.	15.	16.
	84	83	75	95	96	82	76	74
	43	24	45	16	56	34	13	26
	44	94	42	84	66	95	94	76
	45	42	85	54	26	36	14	42
	76	76	92	81	86	95	75	92
	83	43	36	45	46	31	23	63
	95	16	35	96	92	71	73	95
	14	15	25	53	13	62	53	67
	26	74	81	81	78	84	84	94
	54	34	45	16	16	14	11	46
279)		310)	341)	372)	403)	434)	465)	496)

10-Key Touch Key

17.	18.	19.	20.	21.	22.	23.	24.
94	82	91	96	37	18	19	19
66	22	64	45	21	26	23	22
95	84	94	11	18	39	38	38
32	26	21	53	64	42	63	45
86	87	81	95	59	59	58	58
24	46	31	16	45	61	32	62
81	95	71	86	49	59	58	18
23	63	55	36	54	22	21	23
96	86	65	74	28	39	85	33
34	34	64	21	21	56	43	17
527)	558)	589)	620)	651)	682)	713)	744)

25.	26.	27.	28.	29.	30.	31.	32.
47	28	67	39	28	29	19	37
41	16	45	63	31	26	25	66
59	69	59	29	49	38	19	38
65	46	14	53	12	55	14	61
58	57	29	69	57	47	19	49
56	62	32	61	26	11	32	65
67	19	67	69	38	57	39	59
51	25	62	35	13	56	36	25
49	28	59	37	59	59	29	59
66	31	62	31	46	66	34	36
775)	806)	837)	868)	899)	930)	961)	992)

Lesson 5 Answers to Selected Problems

Exercise 1
1. 7 3. 91 5. 29 7. 52 9. 55 11. 88 13. 65 15. 59 17. 38 19. 4 21. 8

Exercise 2
1. 546 3. 528 5. 366 7. 416 9. 564 11. 561 13. 575 15. 516 17. 631 19. 637 21. 396 23. 440 25. 559 27. 496 29. 359 31. 266

Comprehensive Speed and Accuracy Exercise

1-Minute Addition Timing (Keys 1 through 9, 0, 00, minus, and decimal keys)

1. 45.8236	2. 452.024	3. 4.76544	4. 8900.76	5. 7.77750	6. 3942.00	7. − 6000.12	8. 8.17001
−90.6321	765.781	2.55350	7090.62	6.45500	7685.00	6900.03	7.79003
93.1001	−890.209	−7.46100	8070.41	9.34650	6251.00	−1075.61	−9.16002
83.1657	197.390	1.56700	−7460.83	1.69995	8876.00	3009.37	4.13501
33.4987	356.041	2.97480	−9010.94	4.57359	4210.76	8000.79	8.19044
83.9824	919.819	−1.95009	8040.55	−8.34229	3230.58	2401.00	−7.71004
48.7693	−238.816	9.43006	6400.63	4.67899	3790.03	3068.00	3.77007
1073.68	731.921	7.86100	5700.43	6.45775	3260.04	5002.01	9.23004
−90.3213	535.001	4.37300	8800.81	−8.54900	−2110.06	6079.09	5.31005
43.5629	311.321	5.36600	9899.62	3.34556	−9233.06	5006.72	6.48193
83)	166)	249)	332)	415)	598)	581)	664)

9. 1140.61	10. 576.985	11. −756.987	12. 9400.79	13. 4004.51	14. 565.661	15. 200.905	16. 3420.48
662109	346.677	760.122	−9400.79	1300.95	454.012	100.013	−8242.08
5585.31	663.753	−865.455	8200.66	4009.95	−679.867	520.064	4780.06
4115.09	776.988	170.403	4300.50	2072.29	−469.140	−900.014	3483.43
−7742.01	988.565	922.939	9500.55	3007.59	876.442	180.045	9602.45
−8868.43	984.322	359.962	−9500.55	6009.99	865.111	227.128	−1433.31
5159.99	197.759	165.880	6700.72	3005.77	356.341	328.990	2952.42
6662.45	621.002	920.432	7700.50	−2006.59	252.966	−100.053	1678.71
1725.61	−440.005	513.119	9400.95	4006.95	329.854	623.024	3431.24
4137.41	−434.575	233.480	8300.95	−2009.86	952.814	867.711	5461.19
747)	830)	913)	996)	1079)	1162)	1245)	1328)

Comprehensive Speed and Accuracy Exercise Answers to Selected Problems

1. 45.8236	3. 4.76544	5. 7.7775	7. -6000.12
−90.6321	2.5535	6.455	6900.03
93.1001	−7.461	9.3465	−1075.61
83.1657	1.567	1.69995	3009.37
33.4987	2.9748	4.57359	8000.79
83.9824	−1.95009	−8.34229	2401
48.7693	9.43006	4.67899	3068
1073.68	7.861	6.45775	5002.01
−90.3213	4.373	−8.549	6079.09
43.5629	5.366	3.34556	5006.72
1324.6293	**29.47971**	**27.44355**	**32391.28**
9. 1140.61	11. -756.987	13. 4004.51	15. 200.905
6621.09	760.122	1300.95	100.013
5585.31	−865.455	4009.95	520.064
4115.09	170.403	2072.29	−900.014
−7742.01	922.939	3007.59	180.045
−8868.43	359.962	6009.99	227.128
5159.99	165.88	3005.77	328.997
6662.45	920.432	−2006.59	−100.053
1725.61	513.119	4006.95	623.024
4137.41	233.48	−2009.86	867.711
18537.12	**2423.895**	**23401.55**	**2047.82**

PART 3

More

APPLYING YOUR TEN-KEY SKILL

Using the Windows® Calculator

Using the Windows Calculator

Once you have learned to ten-key by touch using Touch Key software, you can use your new skill to solve everyday math problems using the Windows Calculator, which is included with Windows software. Some practice problems are included in this section to help you get started.

The Windows Calculator may be accessed by choosing Start, Programs, Accessories, Calculator. Select View on the Calculator menu bar and make sure Standard is selected.

The Windows Calculator

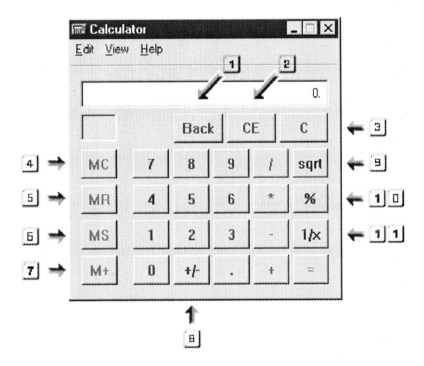

Figure 26

Function Keys

In addition to the numberpad keys you have already learned, keyboard equivalent keys (listed in **Table 7**) are used to perform certain functions. Take a few moments to locate each of these on the keyboard.

When using the Windows Calculator, clicking on the appropriate key with the mouse may also access these function keys. (see **Figure 26**).

	Function	Keyboard Equivalent Key	Description
1	Back (backspace)	← Backspace	Removes the last digit of the displayed number.
2	CE (clear entry)	Delete	Clears incorrect numbers to allow correct re-entry.
3	C (clear all)	Esc	Clears the current calculation.
4	MC (memory clear)	Ctrl + L	Clears any number stored in memory.
5	MR (memory recall)	Ctrl + R	Recalls the number stored in memory. The number remains in memory.
6	MS (memory store)	Ctrl + M	Stores the displayed number in memory.
7	M+ (memory add)	Ctrl + P	Adds the displayed number to any number already in memory.
8	+/- (reverse)	F9	Changes the sign of the displayed number.
9	sqrt (square root)	Shift + @	Calculates the square root of the displayed number.
10	% (percentage)	Shift + %	Displays the result of multiplication as a percentage. Enter 1st number, *, 2nd number, and %. If you use any operator other than the *, the calculator assumes that you meant *, and multiplies the number.
11	1/x (reciprocal)	r	Calculates the reciprocal of the displayed number.

Table 7

Calculator Practice

Key the numbers and operators as shown below. If you key an incorrect number, use Backspace or Delete.

Clear the register with the Clear All (C) key, if necessary.
1. Addition: 474 + 414 =
2. Subtraction: 525 - 258 =
3. Multiplication: 636 x 696 =
4. Division: 696 / 63 =
5. Percentage: What is 10% of 528?
   Solve: 528 x 10 % (or) 528 x .10 =
6. Multiplication and Division with Decimals: Enter all decimal places when multiplying or dividing. If rounding is necessary, round the final result only.
   a. Solve: 1.125 x $75.23 =
      Mentally round your answer to two decimal places:
   b. Solve: $580 / 2.333 =
      Mentally round your answer to two decimal places:
7. Average: 15.95, 11.99, 25.49, 22.50 and 35.00.
   Solve: 15.95 + 11.99 + 25.49 + 22.50 + 35.00 =
   / 5 =

8. Price Increase and Total Price: Raise the unit price by 10%. Find the total price resulting from the price increase.

Quantity	Description	Current Unit Price	New Unit Price	Total Price
74	Part #357	.69		

   a. Solve (Short Method):

      .69 x 1.10 =   x 74 =

   b. Solve (Long Method):

      .69 x .10 =

        + .69 =

        x 74 =

9. Percent of Increase or Decrease

   FIRST, find the <u>amount</u> of the increase or decrease by subtracting.

   SECOND, find the <u>percent</u> of the increase or decrease. To do this, divide by the sales figure for the earlier date (1998).

	Sales 1998	Sales 1999	Amt of Inc./Dec.	Percent of Inc./Dec
Jan.	15,000,000	25,500,000		
Feb.	19,900,550	18,750,000		

   a. Solve: 25,500,000 - 15,000,000 =

      ÷ 15,000,000 =

      Mentally convert to a percent

   b. Solve: 18,750,000 - 19,900,550 =

      ÷ 19,900,550 =

   Mentally convert to a percent and round to 2 decimal places.

10. Calculating a Semester Grade: The grades and their assigned weighting for a student are as follows. Calculate the semester grade.

   Activity   Grade Weight

   Test 1   89   25%

   Test 2   93   25%

   Lab   96   15%

   Project   90   15%

   Final Exam 82   20%

   Solve: 89 * .25 = M+

   93 * .25 =   M+

   96 * .15 =   M+

   90 * .15 =   M+

   2 * .20 =   M+

   MR

Solutions to Windows Calculator Practice

1. 888
2. 267
3. 442,656
4. 11.04761904762
5. 52.8
6.a. 84.63375 $84.63
6.b. 248.6069438491 $248.61
7.   110.93   22.186
8a. .759 $56.17 (rounded)
8b. .069   .759 $56.17 (rounded)
9.a. 10,500,000   .7   70%
9.b. -1,150,550   -.05781498501298   -5.78%
10. 22.25
     23.25
     14.4
     13.5
     16.4
     89.8

PART 4

MORE
APPLYING YOUR TEN-KEY SKILL

Completing Spreadsheets

Data Entry in Spreadsheets

Six partially completed spreadsheet files are included on the Touch Key CD. To practice entering data in these spreadsheets, you will need to start Microsoft Excel® software, open one of the spreadsheets, and, referring to the following pages, key numeric data to complete the spreadsheet.

Spreadsheet Instructions

1. Start Microsoft Excel.

2. Select File, Open, change to the CD drive on your computer (usually D:), Select the folder named Spreadsheet.

3. If your instructor wishes you to save a completed spreadsheet, select File, Save As, change the drive to your floppy containing a data disk (usually A:) and type a new filename. Example: mileage2.xls

4. Select one of the following spreadsheets, turn to the corresponding table in this section and key the data into the appropriate cells of the spreadsheet.

    a. Mileage.xls (**Figure 27**)   Mileage Between Toronto and Selected U.S. Cities

After keying the required data in the spreadsheet, select the "Bar Chart" tab at the bottom of the screen to view a bar chart reflecting the data you have just entered.

    b. Budget.xls (**Figure 28**)   Susan B. Anthony Basic Living Expenses, January 1997

After keying the required data, select the "Pie Chart" tab at the bottom of the screen to view a graphical representation of Susan's budget.

    c. Sales.xls (**Figure 29**)   1996 Sales by City & State

After keying the required data, select the "Map USA" tab to view a graphical representation of sales.

    d. Expense.xls (**Figure 30**)   Computers, Etc. Travel Expense Request for Reimbursement

    e. USCanada.xls (**Figure 31**)   United States/Canadian Mileage

    f. Inventory.xls (**Figures 32-34**)   Essentially Yours - Appliances & Furniture for the Home, Store #16 - Inventory, January 31, 19xx

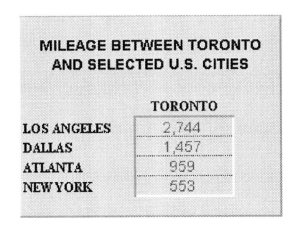

**MILEAGE BETWEEN TORONTO
AND SELECTED U.S. CITIES**

	TORONTO
LOS ANGELES	2,744
DALLAS	1,457
ATLANTA	959
NEW YORK	553

Figure 27 Mileage.xls

**SUSAN B. ANTHONY
BASIC LIVING EXPENSES
JANUARY 1997**

EXPENSE CATEGORY	EXPENSE AMOUNT	% OF TOTAL EXPENSES
Rent	$300.40	31.92%
Utilities	75.10	7.98%
Food	150.00	15.94%
Oil, Gas	69.15	7.35%
Car Insurance	100.00	10.63%
Cable	18.25	1.94%
Car Payment	200.00	21.25%
Phone	28.10	2.99%
TOTAL EXPENSES	$941.00	100.00%

Figure 28 Budget.xls

COMPUTERS, ETC.
1996 SALES BY CITY AND STATE

CITY	STATE	SALES
LOS ANGELES	CALIFORNIA	12,655,456
SAN DIEGO	CALIFORNIA	5,800,500
FRESNO	CALIFORNIA	3,965,710
LAS VEGAS	NEVADA	7,645,958
PHOENIX	ARIZONA	9,850,550
SALT LAKE CITY	UTAH	3,678,832
SANTA FE	NEW MEXICO	2,145,760
DALLAS	TEXAS	7,890,450
HOUSTON	TEXAS	9,345,660
SAN ANTONIO	TEXAS	4,676,500
DENVER	COLORADO	6,098,555
TULSA	OKLAHOMA	2,245,897

Figure 29 Sales.xls

EXPENSE	SUN	MON	TUE	WED	THU	FRI	SAT	TOTAL
Trans. (air)	427.00							427.00
Trans. (rental)								0.00
Trans. (.30/m.)								0.00
Lodging	96.59	96.59	96.59	96.59	96.59	96.59		579.54
Meals	15.30	39.00	28.50	37.91	41.09	22.96	4.55	189.31
Taxi/Limo	10.00						10.00	20.00
Telephone	6.79	4.50	2.20	8.90	7.57	2.39	0.57	32.92
Parking								0.00
Postage		3.00	1.28	10.00	1.60	3.00		18.88
Secretary Serv.		15.00	12.95	22.00	14.75	6.96		71.66
Entertainment		60.99	75.10	123.90	52.13	29.66		349.86
Miscellaneous			4.90	4.90	4.90	4.90		19.60

TOTAL REIMBURSEMENT ⟶ $1,708.77

Figure 30 Expense.xls

UNITED STATES / CANADIAN MILEAGE									
	VANCOUVER	CALGARY	REGINA	WINNIPEG	TORONTO	MONTREAL	MONCTON	HALIFAX	CHARLTTOWN	ST. JOHN'S
LOS ANGELES	1,382	1,692	1,968	2,126	2,744	3,080	3,726	3,861	3,835	4,713
SEATTLE	160	756	1,234	1,591	2,546	2,883	3,522	3,663	3,180	4,509
PHOENIX	1,654	1,543	1,650	1,943	2,069	2,638	3,172	3,345	3,285	4,154
DALLAS	2,255	1,885	1,644	1,335	1,457	1,763	2,256	2,429	23,669	3,238
MINNEAPOLIS	1,694	1,288	811	454	933	1,162	1,801	1,942	1,911	2,788
CHICAGO	2,461	1,735	1,258	900	519	856	1,501	1,636	1,611	2,488
CINCINNATI	2,772	2,046	1,568	1,211	506	824	1,396	1,482	1,506	2,383
DETROIT	2,750	2,023	1,546	1,189	231	568	1,212	1,348	1,322	2,198
ATLANTA	2,825	2,191	1,836	1,554	959	1,240	1,563	1,736	1,676	2,545
TAMPA	3,314	2,823	2,302	2,033	1,396	1,548	1,858	2,031	1,971	2,840
PHILADELPHIA	3,009	2,592	1,885	1,603	503	465	807	980	920	1,789
NEW YORK	3,449	2,699	2,222	1,865	553	383	738	799	846	1,730
BOSTON	3,440	2,714	2,236	1,846	568	341	515	576	624	1,502

Figure 31 USCanada.xls

	A	B	C	D	E	F
1	ESSENTIALLY	YOURS - APPLIANCES AND FURNITURE FOR THE HOME				
2		STORE # 16 - INVENTORY				
3		JANUARY 31, 19xx				
4						
5	ITEM	PRODUCT	VENDOR	UNIT	ITEM	TOTAL
6	DESCRIPTION	NUMBER	NUMBER	COST	QUANTITY	COST
7						
8	Lamps, 12"	17504	10154	9.25	300	2,775.00
9	Lamps, 13"	17514	10154	12.50	26	325.00
10	Track Lighting, 4'	17499	10154	15.50	66	1,023.00
11	Track Lighting, 2'	17498	10154	7.25	145	1,051.25
12	Grow Lamp	17527	10154	19.90	1	19.90
13	Carriage Lamp	17521	10154	13.65	110	1,501.50
14	Door Mats	57789	25122	10.90	1275	13,897.50
15	Oval Rugs 3x5	49791	25122	16.95	121	2,050.95
16	Oval Rugs 2x3	49789	25122	12.30	560	6,888.00
17	Oval Rugs 4x6	49793	25122	20.50	31	635.50
18	Oval Rugs 8x12	49795	25122	30.00	10	300.00
19	Single Box Springs	21232	27156	126.40	30	3,792.00
20	Double Box Springs	21235	27156	134.80	44	5,931.20
21	King Box Springs	21238	27156	151.55	10	1,515.50
22	Single Mattress	31232	27156	139.20	48	6,681.60
23	Twin Mattress	31234	27156	135.50	23	3,116.50
24	Double Mattress	31235	27156	143.21	70	10,024.70
25	King Mattress	31433	27156	148.00	10	1,480.00
26	Amdeck Chairs	79981	22231	29.40	24	705.60
27	Laney Chairs	78882	22231	31.40	21	659.40
28	Single Bed Frame	20015	41713	19.00	5	95.00
29	Twin Bed Frame	20020	41713	19.00	3	57.00
30	Double Bed Frame	20025	41713	22.25	9	200.25

Figure 32 Inventory.xls (continued on next page)

31	King Bed Frame	20030	41713	29.95	6	179.70
32	LXI Stereo	65721	00240	57.00	12	684.00
33	Portable CD	65723	00240	119.00	8	952.00
34	CD Player	65725	00240	214.50	3	643.50
35	Zenith TV 19" color	67556	87442	292.25	5	1,461.25
36	Zenith Console	67575	87442	625.00	3	1,875.00
37	VCR, 2 head	42177	87442	225.00	2	450.00
38	Zenith Large Screen	49002	87442	2,125.75	2	4,251.50
39	VCR, 4 hd., stereo	42172	99250	268.50	2	537.00
40	Zenith 5", b/w	67545	99250	40.50	2	81.00
41	Zenith 9", b/w	61547	99250	49.00	24	1,176.00
42	Zenith 16" color	67552	99250	105.00	10	1,050.00
43	Zenith 19" color	67555	99250	286.00	9	2,574.00
44	Zenith am/fm Radio	60017	99250	33.30	42	1,398.60
45	GE Refrig.-Freezer	57129	31551	420.00	2	840.00
46	GE Refrig. 16 cu.ft.	57122	61551	440.00	3	1,320.00
47	GE Refrig. 20 cu.ft.	57123	31551	870.00	2	1,740.00
48	GE Refrig. 14 cu.ft.	57121	31551	300.00	4	1,200.00
49	Sony am/fm Radio	60006	25127	39.50	11	434.50
50	Sony am Radio	60002	25127	14.45	8	115.60
51	Sony Portable CD	60007	25127	63.00	10	630.00
52	Walkman	60001	25127	6.00	24	144.00
53	Entertainment Ctr.	65701	25127	240.00	2	480.00
54	RCA 19" TV color	67554	25237	280.00	4	1,120.00
55	RCA 21" TV color	67559	25237	340.00	4	1,360.00
56	RCA 25" TV color	67568	25237	490.00	2	980.00

57	RCA VCR, 2 head	42166	25237	1,340.00	3	4,020.00
58	RCA VCR, 4 head	42163	25237	150.00	1	150.00
59						
60			TOTAL INVENTORY COST ⟶			96,574.00
61						

Figure 33 and 34 Inventory, Page 2